My Year of Design TWO

A New Journey of Thinking and Making
for Quilters and other Textile Lovers

Jutta Hufnagel

published by Quilt around the World GmbH

Quilt around the World, My Year of Design TWO, A New Journey of Thinking and Making for Quilters and Other Textile Lovers

© 2017 Quilt around the World GmbH

Quilt around the World GmbH
Jutta Hufnagel
Gross-Nabas-Str. 3
D-81827 Munich
Germany
www.quilt-around-the-world.com

© 2017
Herstellung und Verlag: BoD – Books on Demand, Norderstedt.
ISBN: 978-3-7431-2676-3

Layout and content: Jutta Hufnagel

Editors: Anke B. Calzada, Derry Godden, Johann Gutauer, Jutta Hufnagel

Photos: Quilt around the World GmbH (unless stated otherwise)

Printed in Germany

Table of Contents

The Art History Exercises

The Coincidence Quilt Project

The Block Mystery Quilt Project

The Coincidental Connections

The Line Mystery Quilt Project

Preface

When the original idea for My Year of Design (MYoD) was born in late 2013, little did I anticipate what would become of my design exercises initially meant entirely as my very own challenge and devised to compensate for the impossibility of pursuing a more "academic" path to improve my design capabilities.

A lot has happened since then. The first edition of MYoD was such a success online that we decided to publish the exercises in print and to show a selection of results at the Patchworktage, the annual show organised by the German Patchwork Guild, in 2015.

Feedback from participants and from quilters who had purchased the first My Year of Design book encouraged us to continue this very exciting journey of thinking and making with My Year of Design TWO. Since at Quilt around the World, we always strive to try new things and push the borders wherever possible, My Year of Design TWO introduces a "red thread": art history. This sounds more serious than it really is. The exercises created for My Year of Design TWO continue the "tradition"

of an easy and playful approach, an invitation to step out of well-established design patterns, get off the beaten track, and venture right out into an exciting and creative jungle. The individual exercises need not take up a lot of time to complete while they offer lots of potential to dig deeper, perhaps even create an entire portfolio based on the subject of each art history era.

Ideas continue to flow in and so the My Year of Design familiy has found an even more ambitious sequel in "My Year of Design THREE", a comprehensive online design course offered in three modules focusing on Design Elements, Design Principles and Composition. If you are interested, read more online at My Year of Design THREE:

www.quilt-around-the-world.com/MYoD3

We hope that you will enjoy the exercises in this book as much as our online followers have.

Happy designing!

Jutta Hufnagel

Thank you!

I would like to extend my sincere thanks to...

... **Anke**, **Derry** and **Johann** for supporting the idea of My Year of Design from the very start.

... all the **participant**s who have worked diligently on the tasks and have produced wonderful work for our online gallery and for the exhibitions planned right after the publication of this book. **Your work and your feedback continue to be an immense source of joy and inspiration to me.**

... **Anke**, **Derry**, **Johann** and **Margot** for their patient and constructive proofreading.

... **Anja Koop** (www.anjakoopdesign.de) for her "at all hours" support for everything related to

graphic design.

... **PARTNER MedienWerkstatt UG** for giving us the possibility of showing some of the results of My Year of Design TWO at the Nadelwelt Karlsruhe in June 2016, **Brigitte Höferle** of Stadthalle Erding GmbH who also invited us to present MYoD results to the visitors of the Patchwork and Textilmarkt Erding, one of the largest quilt shows in Southeastern Germany and to Angelika Steinböck of Quilthouse Purgstall, Austria, who opened her shop and classroom for us.

... all **Friends and Supporters** who generously helped to make this publication possible.

Working with this Book

What this Book Offers

*Milwaukee Art Museum
Santiago Calatrava*

Since you have this book in your hands already, it is very likely that you share our desire to experiment, to think outside the box occasionally or even frequently and to question "what has always been done like this". My Year of Design TWO lets you be curious and adventurous and invites you to join us on a creative trip back in time - a new journey of thinking, designing and making.

My Year of Design TWO is a workbook in the truest sense and meant for all quilters of all levels. No matter whether you make art quilts or craft quilts, there is always room for developing new ideas and new approaches.

Each chapter is organised around one of the 18 themes which are loosely based on eras in art history deliberately presented in a non-chronological order.

My Year of Design would like to give you wings and not catapult you back to school.

You are entirely free in your design decisions. The exercises offer a helping and sometimes guiding hand to look at concepts, ideas, your surroundings etc. from a different angle and to question your likes and dislikes from time to time. You are always encouraged to take up the challenge and, at the same time, take the freedom to bend the "rules" to suit your own design.

Never Only One Path...

... to Rome and this also applies to My Year of Design. Two approaches are offered - one gives more support while the other lets you roam freely, guided only by your own assocations and ideas.

1. The Exercise Guideline

The Exercise Guideline offers support and material to guide you through the major concepts of the art history era which is the theme of the chapter you are working on.

My Year of Design TWO does not attempt to be a comprehensive manual on art history. We concentrate on major design aspects and on ideas and concepts which might be useful. In short: We take from each era what is most interesting to a maker of textiles today and leave most of the "Who's who" to the art historians.

Get in the Mood

Every chapter starts with a "Get in the Mood" task. It is meant to introduce the monthly theme in a leisurely manner leaving lots of space for playing around with design ideas without investing too much time and material.

Dig Deeper

"Dig Deeper" gives you a combination of smaller tasks and information to invite you to do just that:

- dig deeper into the main concepts, artistic developments and styles of a specific era in art history and
- be inspired by whatever surprises you in the most unusual places and
- go play with whatever interests and captivates you most.

We have put the exercises in boxes with grey dotted borders to make them easily recognizable.

We encourage you to use this book as a very personal workbook - add your own thoughts, ideas, inspiration, associations, and sketches to whatever we have started for you!

For your work with "Dig Deeper", we recommend that you consider the following five stages on your creative journey:

Association

Note down whatever comes to mind first. You might want to leave your desk or your computer and lie on the sofa or sit on your favourite chair to be as physically and mentally free and comfortable as possible.

Whatever you write down need not be "correct" or historically accurate! The more spontaneous, far-flung, even erratic your first associations are, the more interesting your journey will be.

Questions

Ask yourself questions about the subject. Consult your collection of free associations and select a few areas which seem unclear.

Research

Do some research and find answers to your questions.

Focus on arts and crafts. What materials were used and what techniques became important? Search for particular works of art or craft. Why were these objects of art and craft made during this period?

Consider purchasing a comprehensive book on art history. Museum websites and Wikipedia are excellent online sources.

Selection

Let the results of the previous stages simmer for a few days. Then take out your notes again.

Highlight the aspects which you find most interesting/intriguing/inspiring. Look for areas where your jottings or notes differed from the results of your research. Where there any surprises? Anything unexpected?

Finally, decide on one or two aspects to translate into a design.

Design

Make a design for a block or a (small) quilt using the ideas and material you have collected during the previous stage.

If you are thinking of making a Dig Deeper series, consider using similar formats for your design. Keep the option of making a three-dimensional piece on your long list.

Send us a picture of your final piece along with a comment on your inspiration and how and why you decided on this particular idea (info@quilt-around-the-world.com). We'll publish them in the MYoD2 online gallery.

Always remember that My Year of Design is for you and for you alone:

- Don't think that you have to tackle ALL the exercises and in the given order.

- Do the exercises that interest you most and which fit into your schedule. If time is scarce, consider stopping at the design stage and just sketch what you might make some time in the future.

- Decide on one of the approaches explained above, switch between them as you go through the chapters or concentrate on one type of exercise first and come back later to tackle the rest - just as you please!

- Don't skip parts of the exercises just because they ask for something which you don't like or consider difficult. This might be just what will help you learn and grow the most!

- MYoD2 starts with an analysis of your current situation as a quilter or textile lover (see page 10). Do take the time to complete the sheet - we will come back to what you have noted here later.

2. The Worksheet

If you prefer to work more independently, we offer the My Year of Design TWO Worksheet in the appendix.

The Worksheet maps out the stages of the Exercise Guideline on one sheet without any additional supporting material.

If you work in an office, put the sheet under your keyboard and think about the exercise whenever you have an "island of time". If you work at home, put the sheet on the kitchen table or where you pass it frequently. Use the sheet to make sketches and notes, staple or glue cutouts or pictures etc.

The Playground: Coincidence and Mystery

Thinking and making is hard work and so you will find some fun activities at regular intervals to relax and amuse you.

In the "Coincidence Quilt Project", all basic design decisions (format, layout, design elements, colours, patterns, techniques) for the Coincidence Quilt will be made by rolling a dice. Behind each face lies a design element which will dictate what is to be used in your design.

The "Coincidence Quilt Project" is divided into 10 parts (see Table of Contents).

The "Coincidental Connections Project" defines connections between individual, in this case rectangular, blocks and a set of rules indicating how to connect these "marks". Both the interfaces and the set of rules is again determined by rolling a dice.

The objective of the Coincidence Projects is to collect design instructions which you probably wouldn't have chosen yourself or - even better - seem, at first glance, to be impossible to combine.

Challenges and difficult situations make us stretch and grow, in real life as in quilting!

The "Coincidental Connections Project" is divided into 8 parts (see Table of Contents).

The "Mystery Block Quilt Project" brings you somewhat mysterious instructions for a quilt block - either a traditional block or a block which the Quilt around the World team has designed for you.

The "Mystery Block Quilt Project" has 12 parts (see Table of Contents).

The "Line Mystery Quilt Project" is just that - a photo reduced to a line drawing and chopped into equally sized pieces. There are very few instructions regarding colours, colour values and textures, so again lots of scope for thinking and then making your very own version.

The Mystery Projects invite you to travel to uncharted territory, be adventurous and enjoy the freedom of inventing your own "story".

Throw certainty and security overboard and have fun! There is no right or wrong and the more answers you find to the riddles the better!

The "Line Mystery Quilt Project" has 6 parts (see Table of Contents).

No Gallery?

You will find no gallery of finished pieces based on the My Year of Design TWO exercises in this book. This might be surprising as there are quite a lot of marvellous designs out there created by participants of the online version.

We have deliberately left out pictures of finished My Year of Design TWO results because we would like to give you the opportunity to think first only about what YOU are going to do with what My Year of Design has to offer. We would like to give you the space and the independence to find your own path instead of peeking at other quilters' work when no immediate inspiration hits your creative system.

However, whenever you find yourself at a point where you really need to see other approaches to the My Year of Design exercises, you can have a look at the My Year of Design online gallery at www.quilt-around-the-world.com. Here we have published pictures of all the finished pieces we know of.

The exhibition catalogue for the My Year of Design Travelling Exhibition is also available on CD-ROM. Please go to the Appendix (page 132) for ordering information.

You are more than welcome to keep in touch with us and send us pictures of the work you create based on this book. We would love to publish whatever you make in the My Year of Design online gallery for others to see and to admire.

Black & White

This is meant to be a workbook in the truest sense. Therefore, we have kept the entire layout in black and white to act as backdrop for your creativity. We invite you to write and draw right onto the pages of this book and make it as much your own personal "travel diary" as possible.

Getting Started

You need very little equipment for your journey of thinking and making.

It could be as little as a pencil and a sketchbook (ca. DIN A4 or letter format) and - for the Coincidence projects - a regular dice with 6 numbered sides.

If you like, you could add pens and coloured pencils and a small inexpensive camera which you can take with you wherever you go to record sources of inspiration.

As it is up to you whether and how you put our design impulses into textiles or other media, you will have to decide yourself what materials you need to do this.

If you have trouble deciding on appropriate materials and techniques to "translate" your designs, feel free to e-mail us.

The Very First Exercise

There is one exercise which you should absolutely not skip. This is the mind map on the next page. Take the time to fill in the spaces and occasionally revisit this page. It will be interesting to see whether working on the My Year of Design changes how you look at colours, techniques, your personal likes and dislikes etc.

A Final Note

We have crafted these exercises with lots of love. And it has taken us considerable time to find the right wording, do research, and consult many books on art and design.

We ask you to be fair and not pass these exercises on to your friends. Tell them about My Year of Design, show them what you are making, but please ask them to buy this book to help us continue our work.

We are thrilled that you are interested in taking part and are looking forward to seeing the results of your journey of thinking, designing and making.

Where I am today

We have prepared the beginnings of a mind map for you. Please complete it - either using words written with a pen or using coloured pens to illustrate the mind map with blotches of colour and small sketches. And while you are at it, why don't you replace the grey smiley by a self portrait (as a sketch, a collage etc.)?

Jot down or draw whatever comes to mind first. Then put the MYoD book aside and after a few days go over the list again. If you feel that there is need for revision, DO NOT ERASE anything you have written or drawn during the first visit and DO NOT MAKE a "pretty" version on a newly printed sheet. If anything needs to be crossed out, it should still be legible afterwards.

We will come back to this page occasionally throughout the year. Therefore it is really important that you populate all the branches of your mind map.

My favourite colours

My least liked colours

My favourite materials

My least liked materials

My favourite techniques

My least liked techniques

This is how I usually work

This is something I have never tried before

This is something I would like to try

My creative goals

My creative motto

The Stone Age

Get in the Mood - Stones

The Stone Age is called Stone Age because mankind started to use tools, mostly crafted from stones, in that period. Imagine what a progress it must have been to be able to use a sharp cutting tool to make clothing, to hunt, to cut up fire wood or food!

Stones still have an immense importance in our modern lives which couldn't be farther away from what our Stone Age ancestors knew.

So take this book or your sketchbook and your camera and go out into the countryside, the city centre, a museum, a building supply store or wherever you are likely to find different kinds of stone or stone surfaces.

The more diverse these stones or stone surfaces are, the better.

Examine the stones carefully, look at them closely, and, if possible, touch their surfaces. Make notes in the empty space on this page or in your sketchbook describing and/or sketching the different surfaces. You could even make rubbings using a soft pencil. Take pictures to support your notes.

Back home, leave your notes and pictures for a few days.

Then take up your notes and use them as a basis for designing a block or small quilt.

Try to integrate two or three different textures and think about how you could interpret them to become a pattern in your work. Think about techniques and materials which could help you express the texture of stone in a textile environment.

Texture describes how a surface feels or is perceived to feel. Texture can invite or repel the desire to touch.

If texture appears in a repeating and more or less regular rhythm, it can become a pattern.

Dig Deeper - The Stone Age

Here you will find the beginnings of a mind map including thoughts, questions and some information.

Jump right in and add your own thoughts, inspiration, ideas, perhaps doubts and use your pens and pencils to make this into your personal Stone Age portfolio of ideas and potential textile projects!

Association

really long ago!

The Stone Age is a prehistoric period which ended between 6000 BC and 2000 BC (depending on the source!).

What do you find most interesting about the Stone Age?

dinosaurs?

nobody really <u>knows</u>!

rituals

cult

hunting

animals

Questions

Stick Figures

When looking at drawings made by our Stone Age ancestors, it is amazing how clearly animals and human figures can be recognized although the drawings aren't that detailed. The animals and human figures were reduced to their most important characteristics.

Can you do the same? Draw a herd of bison and a group of hunters only using short pencil strokes.

Which techniques would you use to translate your stick figures onto textiles?

Finger Colours

When did you last use finger paints? Not since you were small?

Then get out your textile paints and, using only your fingers, paint a wolf, a mammoth and a dinosaur.

Research

drawing

cave

earth colours

Neanderthals were people, too

During the Stone Age, humans and their predecessors learnt to craft tools from stone.

What was it like to live in those times?

tools

flintstones

The Stone Age ended when prehistoric "technology" introduced first bronze and then iron for tool making.

What were the major new developments and achievements of humans during the Stone Age?

Selection

3D Stones

How could you make a three-dimensional version of a stone or a rock entirely from fabric?

Design

Learn more online:

en.wikipedia.org/wiki/Stone_Age
en.wikipedia.org/wiki/List_of_Stone_Age_art
humanorigins.si.edu/evidence
www.deutsches-museum.de/en/exhibitions/materials-production/altamira-cave/
www.britannica.com/EBchecked/topic/567232/Stone-Age

Real Places to Visit:

Altamira Cave, Spain
Lascaux Cave, France
Carnac, France
Deutsches Museum, Munich, Germany
The Neolithic Settlement of Skara Brae, Scotland
Stonehenge, near Southampton, England
Neanderthal Museum, Mettmann, Germany

Coincidence Quilt Project - Part 1

Need a break? Here we have a fun distraction for you - the first part of the My Year of Design TWO Coincidence Quilt Project!

The first part of the Coincidence Quilt Project will determine the format of whatever you are going to make.

Remember: All basic design decisions (format, layout, design elements, colours, patterns, techniques...) for your Coincidence Quilt will be made by rolling the dice. Whatever face your dice shows results in the design decisions listed below. Don't cheat yourself out of a personal challenge by throwing the dice until it shows something you like - the objective of this project is to deal with potentially difficult design requirements! Bear in mind that this is first and foremost meant as a design exercise and not as a par force session of extreme sewing.

We are offering two levels. The first level gives you straightforward instructions. The second level builds upon the first and raises the bar one or two notches...

First Level

1   Make a wall hanging, ca. 20" x 30" or 50 x 70 cm.

2   Make a table runner, ca. 12" x 40" or 30 x 100 cm.

3   Make a bed quilt, at least 50" x 70"

4   Make a three-dimensional object, ca. 16" x 16" x 16" or 40 x 40 x 40 cm

5   Make a bag (size optional)

6   Joker: Choose from 1, 2, 3, 4, or 5.

Second Level

1   Whatever you make, it must consist of two parts which can be used/viewed together or independently of each other.

2   Whatever you make, it must have an irregular shape, i.e. "classic" formats are not allowed.

3   Whatever you make, it must have a purpose which you would not expect in a textile.

4   Whatever you make, it must have at least one hole in its surface.

5   Whatever you make, it must be reversable, ie. it must have two viewable/usable sides.

6   Joker: Choose from 1, 2, 3, 4, or 5.

Just because it's fun, it's not necessarily art.

Heidemarie Mönkemeyer

Mystery Block Quilt - Part 1

Have you already reached the final stages of your Stone Age project? Is it difficult to decide on the one aspect you would like to base your final design on?

To relax your brain, take a break and join us in the Mystery Block Quilt project!

The objective of the Mystery Block Quilt is to invite you on a journey where the path to be travelled is not immediately visible. There is no right or wrong in the outcome and the goal is not to "guess" correctly, but to invite insecurity as a chance to create something new.

You will find the solution to this block riddle on page 22.

Here are the instructions based on a traditional block:

1. The block contains 44 pieces.

2. All pieces are the same shape, in three different sizes.

3. At least three different fabrics or colour values should be used.

4. Depending on the colour placement, the overall block design can show either a square on point or a horizontal square.

5. Provided that the sewing order is followed, the block is fairly easy to make.

Every block of stone has a statue inside
and it is the task of the sculptor to discover it.

Michelangelo

Detailed patterns for all Mystery Blocks of this series are available on the exhibition catalogue CD which was produced for the My Year of Design TWO travelling exhibition. For ordering information, please go to the Appendix (page 132) or to our website:

www.quilt-around-the-world.com

The Renaissance

Get in the Mood - Perspective

Take up your sketchbook or use the empty space on this page and draw a horizontal line. On this line, choose one point which will serve as point of reference.

Now make a design based on your horizon and your point of reference. Use different shapes, blocks etc. in different sizes to create the impression that some are farther away than others.

If you have the time, make more than one sketch using different horizons, points of references, shapes or blocks. Then put away your sketchbook and let your ideas and designs simmer for a few days.

Take up your drawings again and select one to turn into a block or a small quilt.

Perspective means that an artist represents an object on a flat surface, e. g. paper, a canvas, or a quilt, as it is seen by the eye.

There are different types of perspectives, depending on how many points of reference there are.

If you are interested, you can read more on Wikipedia:

http://en.wikipedia.org/wiki/Perspective

And why is this relevant for the Renaissance? It's not that the Renaissance artists "invented" perspective. The Greeks and the Romans already used perspective in their art. But it was during the Renaissance that the scientific groundwork was established.

By the way: According to the people in the know, this scientific approach also marked the emancipation of the artists from the craft guilds they belonged to before!

Dig Deeper - The Renaissance

Association

What period preceded the Renaissance and how did the Renaissance differ?

The Renaissance is attributed to the 15th and 16th centuries.

rise of the modern world

What were the major new developments and/or achievements of humans during the Renaissance?

science

the printing press

books

humanistic ideas

The Renaissance is considered to be the starting point of Modern History.

mankind as focus

Questions

Golden Ratio

The Golden Ratio is an important mathematical ratio which is given when the ratio of two quantities is the same as the ratio of their sum to the larger of the two quantities. The Golden Ratio is represented by the Greek letter φ and its value is 1.62 (rounded to two digits).

Can you design a block or a quilt where you apply the Golden Ratio at least three times?

Would you like to have lived in those times?
What do you think would have been the challenges?

Florence

The Renaissance originated in Italy and then spread to the rest of Europe.

Sistine Chapel

Leonardo

Research

perspective

oil paints

sfumato

Far away...

Can you think of other ways to create the illusion of objects being farther away in a quilt or other textile piece?

Think about what effects the choice of colours, materials, techniques etc. could achieve.

Botticelli

Selection

Venus Wanted

One of the most famous paintings of the Renaissance is "The Birth of Venus" by Sandro Botticelli. The original can be admired in the Uffizi in Florence, Italy.

We tampered a little with this painting and removed Venus from the shell from which she has just emerged.

Replace Venus by someone or something which could emerge from the shell today!

How is the Renaissance reflected in today's thinking and making?

Design

Learn more online:

en.wikipedia.org/wiki/The_Renaissance
en.wikipedia.org/wiki/Renaissance_art
www.polomuseale.firenze.it/en/index.php
www.britannica.com/ebchecked/topic/497788/renaissance-art

Real Places to Visit:

Florence, Pisa, Rome and many other places in Italy
Prado Museum, Madrid
Indianapolis Museum of Art, Indianapolis, USA
The Pushkin State Museum of Fine Arts, Moscow

Coincidence Quilt Project - Part 2

How is your Renaissance project going? If you need a fun distraction, get out your dice and continue with the MYoD2 Coincidence Quilt Project!

The second part of the Coincidence Quilt Project will determine the layout of whatever you are going to make.

If you have missed the background information on the coincidence quilt project, please go back to pages 8 and 15.

If you are uncertain about what exactly is behind the instructions, don't hesitate to e-mail us at info@quilt-around-the-world.

First Level

1 Horizontal layout

2 Diagonal layout

3 Medallion layout

4 Strip layout

5 One-patch layout

6 Joker: Choose from 1, 2, 3, 4, or 5.

Second Level

1 Whatever layout, break it up so the grid the layout relies on becomes irregular.

2 Whatever layout, break it up so a focal point emerges between the top left corner and the centre of your quilt/object.

3 Whatever layout, break it up with at least one line which is not straight.

4 Whatever layout, combine it with any of the other given layouts.

5 Whatever layout, add a border which takes up the layout on a much smaller scale.

6 Joker: Choose from 1, 2, 3, 4, or 5.

The designer must think first, work later.

Ladislav Sutnar

Mystery Block Quilt - Part 2

Have you already reached the final stages of your Renaissance project? Is it difficult to decide on the one aspect you would like to base your final design on?

To relax your brain, take a break and join us in the Mystery Block Quilt project!

If you have missed the background information to the Mystery Block Quilt, please go back to pages 8 and 16.

You will find the solution to this block riddle on page 28.

Here are the instructions based on a block designed for you by the Quilt around the World team:

1. The block's design is based on six concentric squares, set on point. Squares 2, 3, 4, 5, and 6 serve as "frames" to the 1st square.

2. The block is symmetrical in all directions.

3. The three inner concentric squares form complete shapes. Squares 4, 5 and 6 are only fragments.

4. The second and third squares are pieced from two differently sized triangles.

5. You will need at least two different colours in at least two different shades.

Perspective is to painting
what the bridle is to the horse,
the rudder to a ship.

Leonardo da Vinci

This is the solution to the block mystery on page 16.

It is called "Corn and Beans", a traditional block which was first mentioned in a slightly different version by the "Ladies Art Company" in 1897.

Detailed patterns for all the Mystery Blocks in this series are available on the exhibition catalogue CD which was produced for the My Year of Design TWO travelling exhibition. For ordering information, please go to the Appendix (page 132) or to our website:

www.quilt-around-the-world.com

Expressionism

Get in the Mood - Emotions

Before we dig deeper into this chapter's main topic, the art era "Expressionism", let's take a look at the relationship between emotions and creativity, the two major driving forces for artists...

Take up your sketchbook, notebook, quilter's diary or use the space on this page. Make two lists: one with five positive emotions and another with five negative emotions.

- What techniques and what materials could you employ to express emotions in your work?

- What is easier - expressing positive or negative emotions? Spend one or two days thinking about the possibilities.

Then choose one of the emotions and make a block or a small quilt expressing this emotion.

- Why did you choose this emotion?

- Is your quilt a reflection of that emotion or the outcome?

Positive Emotions	Negative Emotions
....	....
....	....
....	....
....	....
....	....

You don't have to be an "artist" to put emotion into your work. Quilts witness what you live through, your feelings, your hopes, and your dreams. No matter whether "traditional", "contemporary", "modern" or "art" - if you don't put yourself into the piece, it will be a soulless arrangement of textile materials.

Be daring and passionate and make the best quilt you can at this moment. Then it will be unimportant if it is art or craft - because it will be great!

Dig Deeper - Expressionism

Association

Expressionism originated in Germany in the early 20th century.

effects of industrialization

World War I

difficult to define

Expressionists sought to express emotions rather than physical reality.

What were the major historic incidences of the time, how would you describe the political climate?

We are becoming

Although we mostly associate Expressionism with painting, there were also poets, musicians, film-makers etc. We have included a poem by Henriette Hardenberg (1884 - 1993). How could it be translated into fabric?

We are becoming (by Henriette Hardenberg)
(1913)

We are becoming magnificent from our wish for freedom.

The body is stretching,

This dragging towards foreboded shapes

gives over-tension.

Heavy hips shiver themselves to longer growth.

In tightening we tremble from inner sentiment -

We are so magnificent in longing that we could die.

anti bourgeois

What were the values of the society the expressionists tried to foil?

primary colours

Core elements of Expressionism are linear distortion, a new concept for beauty, radical simplification of details and daring use of colours.

Simplification

Think about some shapes widely used in patchwork and quilting, i. e. the square, the rectangle (portrait or landscape), the triangle in all its variations, the circle etc.

Take a sheet of paper, draw one of these basic shapes and then add objects which could be simplified to these basic shapes, e. g. a square could be a house, but also a car or a dog.

Work on two or three shapes. Can you tell a story using these shapes? What would a textile piece expressing this story look like?

Shadow Colours - Colour Shadows

Look around you and choose any object that is close by - a bottle, a plant, your face reflected in a window or a mirror, a pen, your computer mouse....

Look closely and analyse the shadows on the object and created by the object. Then make a sketch of the shadows ONLY: Use

- pure yellow for the lightest shadows
- pure red for medium dark shadows and
- pure blue for dark shadows.

Don't worry whether your sketch does or does not resemble the original object!

Leave the sketch for a few days. Then take it up again. Fill in the areas between the shadows with mixtures of the colours.

Which emotion from your lists made during this month's "Get in the Mood" comes closest to the resulting picture? Do you like the outcome? What would the picture look like if your shadows were shades of grey instead of primary colours?

Research

woodcut

The Bridge

Wassily Kandinsky

Franz Marc

Der blaue Reiter

The Scream

Selection

What would the Expressionists make of our world today, almost exactly 100 years later?

Design

Learn more online:

en.wikipedia.org/wiki/Expressionism
www.theartstory.org/movement-expressionism.htm
www.moma.org/explore/collection/ge/artists
www.britannica.com/EBchecked/topic/198740/Expressionism

Real Places to Visit:

Guggenheim Museum, New York, USA
Metropolitan Museum of Art, New York, USA
The Tate, London, UK
Centre Pompidou, Paris, France
MuSeenLandschaft Expressionismus, Bavaria, Germany

Coincidence Quilt Project - Part 3

How is your Expressionist project going? Would you like us to distract you again with the MYoD2 Coincidence Quilt Project?

The third part of the Coincidence Quilt Project will determine the first of several colour choices for whatever you are going to make.

If you have missed the background information on the coincidence quilt project, please go back to pages 8 and 15.

If you are uncertain about what is behind the instructions, e-mail us at info@quilt-around-the-world.

First Level

1 Only use primary colours (yellow, red, blue), but use all of them.

2 Don't use blue.

3 Use at least three shades of purple.

4 Use black, brown and grey.

5 Don't use white.

6 Joker: Choose from 1, 2, 3, 4, or 5.

Second Level

1 Whatever colour choice, add your favourite colour.

2 Whatever colour choice, add your least liked colour.

3 Whatever colour choice, make your colour palette angrier.

4 Whatever colour choice, make your colour palette peaceful.

5 Whatever colour choice, add neon colours.

6 Joker: Choose from 1, 2, 3, 4, or 5.

We never really perceive what colour really is.

Josef Albers

Mystery Block Quilt - Part 3

Again we would like to create a little relaxation and distraction from your Expressionism project: Here is next part of the Mystery Block Quilt!

If you have missed the background information for the Mystery Block Quilt, please go back to pages 8 and 16.

You will find the solution to this block riddle on page 34.

Here are the instructions for a traditional block:

1. The basic pattern is a star which is part of a larger star pattern.

2. Divide your square in 64 equal squares before you start drawing.

3. The pattern is made up of squares which are all the same size and triangles in three different sizes.

4. The four 2nd largest triangles point to the centre of the block.

5. You should use at least three different fabrics (light, medium and dark).

It is important to express oneself
provided the feelings are real
and are taken from your own experience.

Berthe Morisot

This is the solution to the block mystery on page 22.

It is called "Packed Blocks" and was designed by the Quilt around the World team.

Detailed patterns for all Mystery Blocks of this series are available on the exhibition catalogue CD which was produced for the My Year of Design TWO travelling exhibition. For ordering informa-tion, please go to the Appendix (page 132) or to our website:

www.quilt-around-the-world.com

Romanesque Art

Get in the Mood - Arcs

Before we dig deeper into this month's main topic "Romanesque Art", let's look at arcs first...

Arcs are well known to quilters. One of the perennial favourites, the Drunkard's Path pattern, is made up of units which can be combined to a perfect arc.

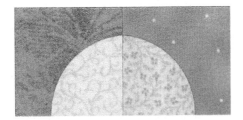

Take this arc block and design a quilt based on this pattern. Remember that you can distort the block, use the block in different sizes, play with colours and fabric patterns etc.

Rounded arches are an important design element in Romanesque architecture. Romanesque churches have clearly defined forms and appear simple especially when compared to the later Gothic buildings. Rounded arches can be found everywhere, not only towards the ceilings, but also in decorative arcading.

The shape of a rounded arch is also a curved line. Lines are important design elements and can be both real and imaginary. A line can also be perceived as the tracing of a travelling point and therefore as the result of movement.

If you are interested to learn more about Design Elements, Design Principles and Composition, you might want to consider taking part in "My Year of Design THREE", an online course split into three modules with 6 chapters each.

For more information, please go to the Appendix (page 133) or to our website:

www.quilt-around-the-world.com/MYoD3

Dig Deeper - Romanesque Art

Association

Rounded arch

Which Romanesque design elements and basic style principles do you like best?

clear and simple

heavy

What were the major historic events of the time, how would you describe the political, social and religious climate?

The Romanesque period lasted from ca. 1000 - 1200.

church vs. "state"

"small people" were not "free people"

Questions

monasteries

Cluny

Santiago de Compostela

The monasteries became the most important centres of art and craft.

Bayeux Tapestry

Textile Stories

The Bayeux Tapestry is one of the most impressive textiles ever created. It is 68 m long and a little over 50 cm high. The embroidery is stitched with wool on linen.

The Bayeux Tapestry depicts the events relating to the battle in Hastings in 1066 which eventually lead to William of Normandy becoming King of England.

If you were to plan a similar project, which event or series of events would you include? Which techniques and which forms of representation would you choose? Is it possible to portray today's events using only abstract motifs?

Research

Would you like to have lived in the Middle Ages? What were the hopes and fears of people then?

Pisa Tower

Nicholas de Verdun

With very, very few exceptions, artists remain anonymous.

What would an illuminated manuscript about our modern life look like?

Illuminated Patchwork

In the Middle Ages, the so-called illumination of manuscripts became very important. Here text is supplemented with initials, borders, miniature illustrations, and gold and silver decoration.

To make your own illuminated patchwork, draw your initials into your sketchbook and adorn them with at least three decorative elements inspired by the medieval manuscripts. How could you translate this into a textile piece? Would you choose "historical" embellishments or would you use a more contemporary approach?

Selection

Neo-Patchwork

Romanesque art was revived 800 to 900 years later in the so-called Neo-Romanesque style.

So, if history repeats itself - which it very often does - we will talk about Neo-Patchwork around the year 2865. What might it look like?

Design

Learn more online:

en.wikipedia.org/wiki/Romanesque_art
en.wikipedia.org/wiki/Romanesque_architecture
www.metmuseum.org/toah/hd/rmsq/hd_rmsq.htm
www.britannica.com/EBchecked/topic/508431/Romanesque-art

Real Places to Visit:

Vézelay, France
Speyer, Germany
Rochester Cathedral, Kent, England
Cathedral Santiago de Compostela, Spain
Pisa Tower, Italy
The valleys of Sousa, Tâmega and Douro, Portugal

Coincidence Quilt Project - Part 4

Again it is time to relax from your design project!

The fourth part of the Coincidence Quilt Project will determine the second of several colour choices for whatever you are going to make.

If you are not familiar with the colour vocabulary below, please read the basic explanation on page 42.

If you have missed the background information for the Coincidence Quilt project, please go back to pages 8 and 15.

First Level

1 Add a very light green to your colour palette.

2 Add a very dark green to your colour palette.

3 Add a very light pink to your colour palette.

4 Add a very dark pink to your colour palette.

5 Add a very light and a very dark yellow to your colour palette.

6 Joker: Choose from 1, 2, 3, 4, or 5.

Second Level

1 Add a complimentary colour to one of the colours already in your colour palette.

2 Add two analogous colours to one of the colours already in your colour palette.

3 Add two triadic colours to one of the colours already in your colour palette.

4 Add a colour which you think works well with the colours already in your colour palette.

5 Add a colour which you think doesn't work well with the colours already in your colour palette.

6 Joker: Choose from 1, 2, 3, 4, or 5.

> If the highest aim of a captain were to preserve his ship,
> he would keep it in port forever.
>
> Thomas Aquinas

Mystery Block Quilt - Part 4

Have you already cleared the final hurdles of your Romanesque project? Have you found an aspect which interests you above everything else?

Perhaps it's now time to relax your brain a little and just play with this block mystery. If you have missed the background information on the Mystery Block Quilt, please go back to pages 8 and 16.

You will find the solution to this block riddle on page 40.

Here are the instructions based on a block designed for you by the Quilt around the World team:

1. The block is made up of 48 pieces.

2. All the pieces are triangles in three different sizes.

3. The general layout is a diagonal.

4. The medium sized triangles are joined to three squares.

5. Jutta would use as many different fabric (scraps) as possible for the smallest triangles. ;-)

About the injunction of the Apostle Paul that women should keep silent in church? Don't go by one text only.

Teresa of Avila

This is the solution to the block mystery on page 28.

It is called "Broken Star", a traditional block pattern first published in 1936 in the Chicago Tribune.

Detailed patterns for all Mystery Blocks of this series are available on the exhibition catalogue CD which was produced for the My Year of Design TWO travelling exhibition. For ordering information, please go to the Appendix (page 132) or to our website:

www.quilt-around-the-world.com

Ancient Egypt

Get in the Mood - Hieroglyphs

The Eye of the Horus, certainly one of the most widely known Egyptian hieroglyphs, has many interpretations: It is a symbol of protection, royal power and good health. Horus was the sky god and its eye was associated with the sun god Ra. The eye was not a passive and receptive organ in Egyptian mythology, but represented action, protection or even wrath. The eye as symbol, therefore, can mean "to make or do" or "one who does".

Take in the theoretical information and look at the Eye of the Horus shown here. Use it as a starting point to create a design. Include at least two of the aspects mentioned above OR put it into a contemporary context.

Consider adding newly created hieroglyphs to express your ideas. What could modern hieroglyphs look like?

Put away your design for a few days. Then take it up again and think about how you could convert your ideas into fabric. Which techniques lend themselves well to depict the Eye of the Horus? Would you use any special materials?

The term "hieroglyph" is derived from Greek and means "the sacred engraved letters". Hieroglyphs are part of the preliterate artistic traditions of Egypt. Egyptian hieroglyphs combine logographic and alphabetic elements, i. e. a symbol can represent both a word and a letter.

Dig Deeper - Ancient Egypt

Association

pyramids

Tutankhamun

What do you find most interesting about Ancient Egypt and its art?

Ancient Egypt is dated by historians to have started around 3150 BC. It ended in 30 BC when Egypt fell to the Romans.

Nile

Geographically, ancient Egypt was concentrated along the River Nile - the area which today is the modern country of Egypt.

Which design elements and basic style principles typical for Ancient Egyptian art interest you most?

no spatial depth in art

Questions

PlanView

When we think about Egyptian Art, most of us probably think about the particular way humans are depicted. Face seen from the side, torso seen from the front, hips and legs again seen from the side.

Perspective is used here to put emphasis on certain aspects of a motif. No unity of perspective is intended. What is considered important is put in plan view.

Now think about your dinner table. In your mind, set the table with your best china, add cutlery, napkins, and even a vase with flowers. Then bring out the food and don't be stingy!

If you were now to sketch a still life in the style of Ancient Egypt, what would your picture look like? What is most important on your dinner table to be put in plan view? Can you make this into a design for a quilt or a quilt block?

mathematics

faience

Ancient Egyptians were gifted builders and they had advanced knowledge of mathematics, medicine and agricultural production techniques.

Research

What were the major historic events of the time, how would you describe the political, social and spiritual climate?

death cult

Atos

Pharaoh

Cleopatra

Napoleon

Selection

Rhythm in Letters

Rhythm is an important part of design, especially if identical or similar design elements are used in one piece. Something which happens frequently in patchwork and quilting! Rhythm is made up of the repetition of design elements and creates a moving and lively order.

If you study lines of text, you might also recognize a rhythm. Break this rhythm as follows and create text without any meaning:

- Write or type a line of text using only tall letters.
- Write or type a line of text using only small letters.
- Write or type a line of text using only rounded letters.
- Write or type a line of text using only spiky letters.

Enlarge your text lines, print several versions and start to play: Make a collage, combine the different patterns created by the letters, consider cutting through the letters horizontally and combining them with a different text line...

How could you use your letter mosaic in a quilt or a quilt block?

Design

Learn more online:

en.wikipedia.org/wiki/Art_of_ancient_Egypt

www.metmuseum.org/toah/hi/te_index.asp?i=14

www.britannica.com/EBchecked/topic/180644/Egyptian-art-and-architecture

www.boundless.com/art-history/textbooks/boundless-art-history-textbook/ancient-egyptian-art-4/

Real Places to Visit:

Egyptian Museum, Kairo, Egypt

British Museum, London, UK

Oriental Institute, Chicago, USA

Ägyptisches Museum Berlin, Germany

Staatliches Museum Ägyptischer Kunst, Munich, Germany

Museo Egizio, Turino, Italy

Coincidence Quilt Project - Part 5

How is your Egyptian Art project going? Again, as in all chapters, it is time to roll the dice again for a little distraction...

The fifth part of the Coincidence Quilt Project will determine the first of several shape aspects for whatever you are going to make.

If you have missed the background information for the Coincidence Quilt project, please go back to pages 8 and 15.

First Level

1   Use at least one star in your design.

2   Use at least three flower motifs in your design.

3   Add at least one animal or some animal traces (e. g. footprints) to your design.

4   Add at least three heart shapes to your design.

5   Use at least one house as motif.

6   Joker: Choose from 1, 2, 3, 4, or 5.

Second Level

1   All shapes selected for this round must be inverted, i. e. the shape is defined by its surroundings.

2   All shapes selected for this round must be three-dimensional.

3   All shapes selected for this round may be silhouettes only.

4   All shapes selected for this round must be outlines only.

5   All shapes selected for this round must be transparent or appear to be so.

6   Joker: Choose from 1, 2, 3, 4, or 5.

The aim of art is to represent not the outward appearance of things, but their inward significance.

Aristotle

Mystery Block Quilt - Part 5

Have you already reached the final stages of your Egyptian Art project? Have you found an aspect which interests you more than everything else?

If you need a break, have some fun and solve this block riddle. If you have missed the background information for the Mystery Block Quilt, please go back to pages 8 and 16.

You will find the solution to this block riddle on page 46.

Here are the instructions based on a traditional block:

1. The block is made up of 68 pieces.

2. There are only four squares in this block. Together with the four surrounding patches, these squares form simple stars.

3. The pattern could be interpreted as a simplified windmill.

4. When placed side by side with the same block, the pattern tesselates and disguises the individual blocks.

5. You will need at least two different fabrics which contrast well.

All great composers of the past spent most of their time studying.
Feeling alone won't do the job. You also need technique.

George Gershwin

This is the solution to the block mystery on page 34.

It is called "April Breeze", a block designed by the Quilt around the World team.

Detailed patterns for all Mystery Blocks of this series are available on the exhibition catalogue CD which was produced for the My Year of Design TWO travelling exhibition. For ordering information, please go to the Appendix (page 132) or to our website:

www.quilt-around-the-world.com

Bauhaus

Get in the Mood - Colour Play

Go back to the mind map you filled in at the very beginning of MYoD2. What did you put there for your least liked colour? Take up this colour and determine its triadic partners on the colour wheel (see also grey box below).

Now use the worksheet provided on page 126. Colour the fields in the first template as indicated on the worksheet. Now use less or more of your least liked colour in the second template. How does the mood of the colour trio change? Does it change the way you see your least liked colour?

We have included two more templates for you to play with. Add other colours and/or repeat the exercise with your favourite colour and its triadic partners.

Which colour chart do you like best?

This "Get in the Mood" exercise was inspired by both Johannes Itten and Josef Albers who taught extensively on colour theory.

Many quilters will tell you that the choice of colour is one of the most important decisions in a quilt. Colour choices can enhance a pattern or drown it. Colour theory is an important part of any art and craft syllabus and many quilt teachers will advise you to use a colour wheel when designing a quilt.

No matter which version you use (an Internet search will provide you with several different wheels), a colour wheel offers several different colour strategies:

Monochromatic Use of Colour

Use only one colour in different shades.

Complementary Colours

Complementary colours lie opposite each other on the colour wheel. This colour strategy works especially well and is always a good option to consider in a quilt.

Analogous Colours

Analogous colours lie side by side on the colour wheel. Depending on the colour wheel you are using, consider choosing three or more neighbouring colours.

Triadic Colours

Triadic colours are three colours which are equidistant on the colour wheel, i. e. they divide the circle into thirds.

Dig Deeper - Bauhaus

Association

Bauhaus

Founded by Walter Gropius in 1919 with the idea of creating a "total work of art in which all arts will be brought together".

What do you find most interesting about the Bauhaus and the ideas and principles it stood for?

unification of art and craft

New Objectivity

Radically simplified forms, rationality and functionality, reconciliation of mass-production with the individual artistic spirit

Colour Wheel

modern furniture

Which design aspects and style principles typical for the Bauhaus do you like best?

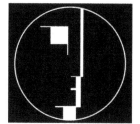

"School of Building"

architecture

Questions

Deutscher Werkbund
("German Association of Craftsmen")

Gestalt psychology

Lines

Select three different black pens or pencils, e. g. a thick marker, a regular felt tip pen and a pen with a very fine tip. On one sheet of paper, draw a line with each of these pens. The lines can be straight or curved, but they should "interact" with each other, i. e. the lines should touch or intersect one or all of the other lines.

If you like, make more than one drawing. Change the order in which you use the pens. Does this make any difference?

Wait a few days and then take up your drawings again. Are there any promising shapes or areas formed by the lines? In what way does the difference in "weight" affect the overall design?

How could the designs be used in a quilt or in a quilt block?

Research

What were the major historic events of the time, how would you describe the political and social climate?

The school was first located in Weimar, moved to Dessau in 1925 and to Berlin in 1932. It had to close under Nazi pressure in 1933.

Abstracted Seasons

Select a simple design element, e. g. a short line, a dot or a small circle, a square etc.

Then use this element to express the four seasons of the year. Use a separate sheet of paper for spring, summer, autumn and winter. Draw your elements with a pencil or a black pen and don't use any coloured pens or pencils. You can use any number of your selected element and you may vary their size. Don't mix different elements in one drawing.

Put away your drawings for a few days. Then take them up again and contemplate your work. Do you still see the seasons of the year in your pictures? In what ways could you translate your sketch into fabric?

Gunta Stölzl

Selection

Wassily Kandinsky

Paul Klee

Tactile Tables

Lazlo Moholy-Nagy, another great artist who taught at the Bauhaus from 1923 until 1928 and who was an important pioneer in photo art, encouraged the students of the so-called "Vorkurs" (foundation course) to compose "tactile tables", i. e. collections of textured materials and to assign them characteristics and also moods and emotions.

Do the same, either with actual pieces of (textile and non-textile) materials and/or with pictures of patterns and textures. How could you make a "tactile table" entirely with fabric? Which techniques could you use?

Would you like to have been a student at the Bauhaus? Which of the workrooms would have interested you most? What would a Patchwork and Quilting Bauhaus look like?

Design

Learn more online:

en.wikipedia.org/wiki/Bauhaus

www.bauhaus.de/en/

www.metmuseum.org/toah/hd/bauh/hd_bauh.htm

www.theartstory.org/movement-bauhaus.htm

Real Places to Visit:

Bauhaus Museum, Weimar, Germany

Bauhaus-Archiv, Berlin, Germany

The Metropolitan Museum of Art, New York, USA

Museum of Fine Arts Bern, Switzerland

Misawa Homes Bauhaus Collection, Tokyo

Coincidence Quilt Project - Part 6

How is your Bauhaus project going? Have you already selected the aspect(s) you will focus your final piece on? If you need a fun distraction, get out your dice and continue with the Coincidence Quilt Project!

The sixth part of the Coincidence Quilt Project will determine more shape choices of whatever you are going to make.

If you have missed the background information on the Coincidence Quilt Project, please go back to pages 8 and 15.

First and Only Level for this Round

1   Include a straight line running from the top to the bottom of your quilt.

2   Include a curved line running from the top to the bottom of your quilt.

3   Include a straight line running from the left edge to the right edge of your quilt.

4   Include a curved line running from the left edge to the right edge of your quilt.

5   Include a diagonal line running from one corner to the opposite corner of your quilt.

6   Joker: Choose from 1, 2, 3, 4, or 5.

Note: The lines can be actual lines, but could also be imaginary, e. g. a border formed by a group of design elements, colour areas etc.

> It cannot be too plainly stated that it is quite unimportant whether photography produces "art" or not. Its own basic laws, not the opinions of art critics, will provide the only valid measure of its future worth.
>
> László Moholy-Nagy

Mystery Block Quilt - Part 6

And here another distraction from your Bauhaus portfolio work.

If you have missed the background information for the Mystery Block Quilt, please go back to pages 8 and 16.

You will find the solution to this block riddle on page 52.

Here are the instructions based on a block designed for you by the Quilt around the World team:

1. The block is made up of 27 sub-units.

2. Each of these sub-units consists of four identical pieces.

3. The sub-units are two different sizes.

If you, unknowing, are able to create masterpieces in colour, then unknowledge is your way.
But if you are unable to create masterpieces in colour out of your unknowledge, then you ought to look for knowledge.

Johannes Itten

This is the solution to the block mystery on page 40.

It is called "Ribbon Quilt" and was first published in the Birmingham News in 1935.

Detailed patterns for all Mystery Blocks of this series are available on the exhibition catalogue CD which was produced for the My Year of Design TWO travelling exhibition. For ordering information, please go to the Appendix (page 132) or to our website:

www.quilt-around-the-world.com

Islamic Art

Get in the Mood - Complex Grids

When we think about Islamic Art, images of intricate geometric designs probably pop up in our minds. Art historians date this "era" from as early as the 5th century (including pre-islamic art) until the 17th century, others conclude with the 16th century.

The intricate patterns which adorn the walls of mosques and palaces are based on complex grids. These grids are often based on various polygons (squares, pentagons, hexagons etc.). The polygons are supported by additional construction lines to help create the final pattern.

Here we have included the grid which is the basis for a pattern in the Great Mosque of Kairouan in Tunisia which was built in 670*.

Use the grid to create your own pattern:

- Highlight lines you would like to use in your design.

- If you want to create a pattern which continues into the next block, you need to take care that the lines touch the outline of your block and begin again on the opposite side.

- Create an outline block or colour the "patches" in different colours.

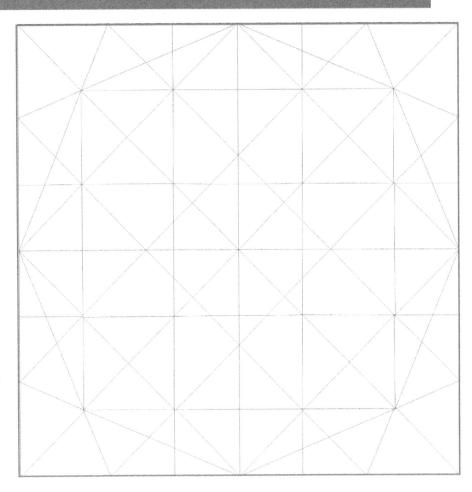

A larger version and a grid including several blocks can be found in the appendix on pages 123 - 124.

*Source for the construction technique and highly recommended further reading: Islamic Geometric Patterns by Eric Broug

Dig Deeper - Islamic Art

Association

arabesque

calligraphy

What do you find most interesting about Islamic Art and the ideas and artwork it is famous for?

Islamic Art is defined as the visual arts produced by artists and craftspeople living in areas ruled by Islamic populations.

no human representation?

Islamic Art is not restricted to religious art and includes secular elements, sometimes even elements frowned upon or forbidden by some Islamic theologians.

The Blue Qu'ran

Hagia Sophia   mosque

Mihrab   Alhambra

Which design aspects, style principles, motifs and objects typical for Islamic Art do you like best?

ceramics

carpets

Questions

Tiles and Tesselations

An important element in Islamic Art are the ceramic tiles and mosaics which cover floors and walls. What is very interesting about tiles in general is the fact that certain geometric shapes will always tesselate with itself while other shapes don't.

The first example is the irregular quadrilateral, i. e. a geometric shape with four corners which is not (necessarily) a square (which would be a regular quadrilateral as it has four identical sides and four identical angles). An irregular quadrilateral will always tesselate with itself.

The second example is a tesselating shape (e. g. a square, a parallelogram, a rectangle etc.) from which you cut out a piece on one side and add this piece to the opposite side.

Use one of these methods and create your own tesselation pattern! Don't think about "sewability" at first - just play with the shapes! When you have developed a design, start working on strategies to translate your pattern into fabric.

Further and highly recommended reading on tesselations: "Designing Tesselations" by Jinny Beyer

Research

Islamic Art builds on many styles already existing, e. g. Roman, Early Christian, Byzantine, Sassanian Art etc.

The Moor's Last Sigh

When Boabdil had to surrender the Alhambra in 1492 to the Spanish rulers Ferdinand and Isabel, legend has it that, from an opposite promonitory, he looked back, sighed in grief at what he had lost and then continued on his journey into exile.

If you had been owner of the Alhambra and had to leave it as Boabdil did, what would you have taken with you? Think about actual things, but also about ideas and dreams...

How could you create a textile memory of the Alhambra?

What are the major historic, social and religious connotations when you think about how and why Islamic Art evolved?

caliphate

expansion

Selection

1492

What are the major contemporary developments in Islamic Art? Is it at all correct to speak of "Contemporary Islamic Art" as a collective?

Contemporary interpretation: Institut du Monde Arabe (Paris)

Penrose Tiling

Go online and research the Penrose tiling.

In what ways could you translate your findings into a textile piece? Which technique(s) would be suitable?

Design

Learn more online:

en.wikipedia.org/wiki/Islamic_art
www.metmuseum.org/toah/hd/orna/hd_orna.htm
www.bbc.co.uk/religion/religions/islam/art/art_1.shtml
www.vam.ac.uk/page/i/islamic-middle-east/

Real Places to Visit:

Great Mosque of Kairouan, Tunisia
Alhambra, Granada, Spain
Institut du Monde Arabe, Paris, France
The Museum of Islamic Art, Qatar

Coincidence Quilt Project - Part 7

Are you making progress with your Islamic Art project? As usual, we have some distraction for you.

The seventh part of the Coincidence Quilt Project will determine patterns and textures to be used in your Coincidence Quilt.

If you have missed the background information for the Coincidence Quilt project, please go back to pages 8 and 15.

First Level

1   Use only solid fabrics for your quilt.

2   Don't use solid fabrics for your quilt.

3   For at least one colour in your quilt, use at least three very differently patterned fabrics.

4   Use at least three different pattern scales in your quilt, i. e. small, medium and large patterns.

5   Use at least one large patterned fabric from which you cut pieces in such a way as to leave one or several motifs intact (also called fussy cutting).

6   Joker: Choose from 1, 2, 3, 4, or 5.

Second Level

1   Use at least three striped fabrics in your quilt.

2   Use at least one check fabric in your quilt.

3   Use at least one polka dot fabric in your quilt.

4   Use at least one fabric with a rose pattern in your quilt.

5   Use at least one photo-print fabric in your quilt (consider printing one of your own photos onto fabric).

6   Joker: Choose from 1, 2, 3, 4, or 5.

> Coincidence reigns everywhere. Just let your fishing rod lie there. When you least expect it, there will be a fish in the maelstrom.
>
> Ovid

Mystery Block Quilt - Part 7

And at the end of this chapter, a little relaxation: the seventh part of the Mystery Block Quilt!

If you have missed the background information for the Mystery Block Quilt, please go back to pages 8 and 16.

You will find the solution to this block riddle on page 58.

Here are the instructions based on a traditional block:

1. This block is very, very well-known and a favourite with many quilters.

2. It consists of four design elements.

3. These design elements form an optical illusion, i. e. the pieces you sew have little to do with the pattern they create.

> There is geometry in the humming of the strings, there is music in the spacing of the spheres.
>
> Pythagoras

This is the solution to the block mystery on page 46.

It is called "Column of Triangles" and was designed by the Quilt around the World team.

Detailed patterns for all Mystery Blocks of this series are available on the exhibition catalogue CD which was produced for the My Year of Design TWO travelling exhibition. For ordering information, please go to the Appendix (page 132) or to our website:

www.quilt-around-the-world.com

impressionism

Get in the Mood - Light Sources

Find a place with different light sources.

This might be a bar or a restaurant with individual lighting at the tables, some lighting over the bar and sunlight or street lighting coming in from the windows. Or enjoy a sunset on a candlelit table with perhaps some diffused city lighting in the background. Broad daylight out of doors is probably the most difficult setting in this case, but even here you might be successful.

There should be at least three light sources which, ideally, should be as diverse as possible (direct light vs. indirect light, precise lighting vs. diffused lighting, white light vs. lights in different colours etc.).

Don't orchestrate the light setting too much - let yourself be guided by what is already there. If necessary, add some candlelight or similar lighting if you feel that the given setting is too simple or doesn't give you enough light sources.

Sit for a while in your chosen setting and analyse where the light comes from and what its characteristics are. Concentrate on the light sources and try to blank out everything else that is surrounding you.

Can you make this into a design for a quilt or a quilt block?

Think about how you can express rays of light vs. diffused light in fabric! Which patterns and/or techniques lend themselves better for the former and which for the latter?

One of the most striking characteristics of Impressionist painting is the emphasis on accurate depiction of light and of accentuating the passage of time by showing light in its changing qualities.

Impressionists pay close attention to the reflection of colours from object to object. Grays and blacks are rarely mixed from pure black, but by mixing together complementary colours.

Dig Deeper – Impressionism

Association

play of light

outdoors

Waterlilies

rebellion

The Impressionists were a group of painters based in Paris who rebelled against the established art community by staging their own independent exhibitions.

Which design aspects, style principles, motifs and objects typical of Impressionism do you like best?

Important aspects are the brushwork (rough, visible, applied with speed), the depiction of light, painting out of doors, choice of motifs (ordinary subjects, unusual visual angles), open compositions, use of colour.

colours

Simultaneous contrast

Pure Colours

Another important characteristic of Impressionist paintings is the way colours are applied to the canvas. Rebellious as the early Impressionists were, they deliberately violated the rules of the "art establishment" of their times. Pure unmixed colours were placed freely and in rough brush strokes without blending or shading.

Can you achieve a similar effect with fabric?

Which techniques and/or patterns would you use to emulate the Impressionist brush strokes in patchwork and quilting? What fabrics would you chose?

immediacy and movement

Questions

spontaneity

Be Spontaneous

Sit down at your workplace, get out your sketchbook and your pen. Then set your timer to 10 minutes.

Make a design for a small wall-hanging which is a summer landscape with meadows and a sky with a few clouds. Your landscape must include at least one flower and two animals.

When the alarm sounds after 10 minutes, stop. Put away your sketch for a few days. Then take it up again and decide what you are going to make.

Research

Pointilisim

Take your sketchbook and select a few pens of different thickness and colours. Then add dots to the blank page:

- Place differently sized dots randomly on your sheet of paper.
- Choose areas where you put more dots than on the rest of the surface.
- Experiment with differently coloured dots.
- Place complimentary coloured dots side by side.

Add dots until you are satisfied with your design.

Put it away for a few days. Then take up your sketchbook again and look at your dots:

Are there areas which seem to jump out at you? What about the colour areas? Would you like to add anything or take anything away?

If you like, make some last changes and then think about how to translate your dots into a textile piece. Which techniques would be suitable? Are there any particular materials which could be useful?

Degas

Monet

Selection

Morisot

From Impressionism, Post-Impressionism evolved which built on the Impressionists' new techniques, but developed yet different approaches regarding colour, pattern, form and line.

Cézanne

What influence has Impressionism had on subsequent eras of art history?

Design

Learn more online:

en.wikipedia.org/wiki/Impressionism

www.metmuseum.org/toah/hd/imml/hd_imml.htm

www.nationalgallery.org.uk/paintings/learn-about-art/guide-to-impressionism/guide-to-impressionism

www.britannica.com/art/Impressionism-art

Real Places to Visit:

Musée d'Orsay, Paris, France

Neue Pinakothek, Munich, Germany

Museo Thyssen-Bornemisza, Madrid, Spain

The Museum of Fine Art, Boston, USA

Courtauld Institute Galleries, London, UK

Coincidence Quilt Project - Part 8

How is your Impressionist project going? Put aside your portfolio for a few minutes and let yourself be distracted a little by the Coincidence Quilt!

The eighth part of the Coincidence Quilt Project will determine which techniques you should use.

If you have missed the background information on the Coincidence Quilt Project, please go back to pages 8 and 15.

First Level

1 Use one of your least favourite techniques.

2 Use reverse appliqué. If you don't know what that is, contact us at info@quilt-around-the-world.com.

3 Use one of your favourite techniques.

4 Use crazy patchwork. If you don't know what that is, contact us at info@quilt-around-the-world.com.

5 Use English Paper Piecing.

6 Joker: Choose from 1, 2, 3, 4, or 5.

Second Level

1 No matter which technique(s) you are using, find a new angle and change it/them.

2 Add a 3D effect to your technique(s).

3 For at least one design element, include tucks and pleats.

4 For at least one design element, use fussy cutting. If you don't know what that is, contact us at info@quilt-around-the-world.com.

5 Include at least one yo-yo in your design. If you don't know what that is, e-mail us at info@quilt-around-the-world.com.

6 Joker: Choose from 1, 2, 3, 4, or 5.

If you shake the tree,
you ought to be around
when the fruit falls to pick it up.

Mary Cassatt

Mystery Block Quilt - Part 8

Of course there is even more diversion from your Impressionist Art project - here is the 8th part of the Mystery Block Quilt!

If you have missed the background information for the Mystery Block Quilt, please go back to pages 8 and 16.

You will find the solution to this block riddle on page 64.

Here are the instructions based on a block designed for you by the Quilt around the World team:

1. This block is a combination of three different basic patterns: You can see a star, at least one square set on point and several curved lines.

2. The overall design is achieved by using four different shapes.

3. Each shape appears only in one size.

4. The total number of pieces is 44.

> The true mystery of the world is the visible, not the invisible.
>
> Oscar Wilde

This is the solution to the block mystery on page 52.

It is called "Card Trick" and and is a very well-known traditional block pattern.

Detailed patterns for all Mystery Blocks of this series are available on the exhibition catalogue CD which was produced for the My Year of Design TWO travelling exhibition. For ordering information, please go to the Appendix (page 132) or to our website:

www.quilt-around-the-world.com

ukiyo-e

Japanese Woodprints

Get in the Mood - Diagonal Compositions

Use this beginnings of an asymmetrical composition as the basis of a design. The two diagonals serve as additional guidelines, but need not play a prominent role in your work.

You are free to do whatever first comes to mind - create a pictorial scene, work with abstract shapes, use elements from traditional patchwork blocks, introduce patterns from other cultural backgrounds (including Japanese influences) etc.

Leave your design for a day or two and then take it up again. Could it be improved? Would you like to add anything or take anything away?

Also consider making two or three spontaneous sketches and taking up the most promising one after one or two days.

In what ways could you translate your design into a textile piece?

Composition in the visual arts is understood as the placement and organisation of "art ingredients" such as line, shape, colour, pattern etc. Japanese art prefers asymmetrical and diagonal compositions placing the viewpoint at unusual angles.

If you are interested in learning more about Design Elements, Design Principles and Composition, you might want to consider taking part in "My Year of Design THREE", an online course split into three modules with 6 chapters each.

For more information, please go to the Appendix (page 133) or to our website:

www.quilt-around-the-world.com/MYoD3

Dig Deeper - Ukiyo-e

Association

Ukiyo-e are woodblock prints (and also paintings) popular in Japan from the 17th through the 19th century.

What are the major historic, social and religious developments of the era when Ukiyo-e was most popular?

Floating World

Edo

Floating World

The Japanese term for the woodprints of the Edo period means "floating world". It reflects the lifestyle in Edo (modern Tokyo) which saw rapid economic growth from the early 17th century onwards. All social classes enjoyed visits to the kabuki theatre and the courtesans and geishas of the pleasure districts were in high demand. A purely hedonistic lifestyle evolved which was reflected in early Ukiyo-e woodprints (and paintings).

What would be the "floating world" of the 21st century?

Think about elements of hedonistic lifestyles in our times. Which images would you include in contemporary Ukiyo-e pieces? Would you prefer to express them in a monochrome setting or use many different colours? In what way could your ideas and concepts for today's Ukiyo-e be translated into fabric?

woodblock

Ukiyo-e pictures show beautiful women in traditional Japanese costumes, actors of the popular kabuki theatre and sumo wrestlers, erotica, and also travel scenes and landscapes.

kabuki

"sex sells"

traditional aesthetics?

Questions

The first Ukiyo-e prints were monochrome pieces. Multicoloured prints became popular in the mid 1700s as new technology became available to the artists and printers.

patterns

Which design aspects, style principles, motifs and objects typical of Ukiyo-e do you like best?

Research

Lines and Faces

The line as a design element plays an important role in almost every piece, whether straight or curved, defining or filling a shape, regular or irregular. In Ukiyo-e, the line is one of the defining features, especially in the early monochrome prints.

For this exercise, we ask you to take out your sketchbook and play with lines. Make at least five sketches of very simple faces (eyes, nose, mouth, possibly some wrinkles) to express joy, fear, surprise, anger and boredom.

Important: Borrowing from the ubiquitous emoticons might be tempting. We suggest, however, that you really try to draw "new" faces.

Any ideas how to integrate your line faces into your textile work?

Hiroshige

Hokusai

The Art of Not Making

This is only about thinking - no making required!

What do you think about the separation of designing and actually making a piece? If the craftsperson or the artist puts all or parts of the creation into other hands, is the outcome still his or her own work? Do you see any difference in craft vs. art? Would you consider just designing a quilt or textile piece and then finding somebody who does the sewing/stitching for you?

Selection

What would Ukiyo-e look like today?

Impressionism and Post-Impressionism

Ukiyo-e art, like all Japanese art, became a major influence in the Western art of the 19th century.

Design

Learn more online:

en.wikipedia.org/wiki/Ukiyo-e

www.metmuseum.org/toah/hd/ukiy/hd_ukiy.htm

www.metmuseum.org/toah/hd/plea/hd_plea.htm

www.britishmuseum.org/explore/highlights/articles/u/ukiyo-e_paintings_and_prints.aspx

www.britishmuseum.org/explore/highlights/articles/u/ukiyo-e_paintings_and_prints-1.aspx

Real Places to Visit:

Ukiyo-e Museum, Matsumoto, Japan

The British Museum, London, UK

Ukiyo-e Ōta Memorial Museum of Art, Tokyo, Japan

Art Institute Chicago, USA

The Museum of Fine Arts, Houston, USA

Rijksmuseum, Amsterdam, Holland

Coincidence Quilt Project - Part 9

Again we have prepared a short and amusing break as a relaxation from your portfolio work:

The ninth part of the Coincidence Quilt Project will again focus on techniques, this time with a focus on embellishments.

If you have missed the background information for the Coincidence Quilt, please go back to pages 8 and 15.

First and only Level

1 Include beads or sequins.

2 Use embroidery stitches OTHER THAN quilting stitches.

3 Add at least one found object to your piece which is in line with other design decisions you have taken previously.

4 Add at least one non-textile item which does not belong to the usual additions in a textile such as buttons, beads etc.

5 Add at least one 3D item as an embellishment.

6 Joker: Choose from 1, 2, 3, 4, or 5.

Katasumuri

sorosoro nobore

fuji-no yama

The small snail

goes up very slowly

Mount Fuji

Kobayashi Issa

Mystery Block Quilt - Part 9

Sit back, relax and have fun with our 9th block riddle!

If you have missed the background information for the Mystery Block Quilt, please go back to pages 8 and 16.

You will find the solution to this block riddle on page 70.

Here are the instructions based on a traditional block:

1. This block consists of four identical smaller blocks.

2. These blocks are made up of identical sub-units in two different sizes.

3. The blocks are asymmetrical and follow a strong diagonal.

4. The total number of pieces is 64.

Keizoku wa chikara nari.
Persevere and never fear.

Japanese Proverb

This is the solution to the block mystery on page 58.

It is called "Circle Star" and was designed by the Quilt around the World team.

Detailed patterns for all Mystery Blocks of this series are available on the exhibition catalogue CD which was produced for the My Year of Design TWO travelling exhibition. For ordering information, please go to the Appendix (page 132) or to our website:

www.quilt-around-the-world.com

Celtic Art

Get in the Mood - Spirals

Fill the spaces within the four spirals with drawings. Use a pencil or a fineliner and "doodle" away. Make sure that you vary the patterns and the themes of your drawings. You are of course free to follow your own imagination, but if you have trouble thinking about anything, we suggest that you fill one spiral with vegetal shapes, one with shapes inspired by animals (including the two-legged species!), one with only straight lines and one with only curved lines.

Put your drawing aside for a day or two. Then take up your work again and think about its possibilities.

Can it be adapted for a textile piece? Which techniques would be especially suitable?

Dig Deeper - Celtic Art

Association

Druids

What do you find most interesting about the Celts and their art?

Hallstatt - La Tène

From an archeological point of view, the Celts are the people who lived in Europe in the Iron Age from ca. 1000 BC until the Romans conquered most of their territory.

Ireland

The term "Celtic Art" covers a much longer period - firstly because large parts of the British Isles were never conquered by the Romans and secondly because the 18th century saw a "Celtic Revival" mostly in Ireland.

Which design aspects, style principles, motifs and objects typical for Celtic Art do you like best?

jewellery

knotwork

Tara Brooch

torcs

Questions

interlacing

Interlace patterns are seen as the most typical representative of Celtic Art and are widely used to this day in illustrations, tattoos, and even computer games placed in the Middle Ages.

Not an Iron Fist, but..

Celtic languages survive to this day, mostly in Ireland, Scotland, Wales and Brittany. However, Celtic languages were spoken all over (continental) Europe before the Romans invaded. Still today, we can find remnants, e. g. in the names of rivers, towns and things we have in daily use.

One of these remnants is the term "isarnon" which has become iron in English and Eisen in German.

What are your first associations regarding iron? What characteristics come to mind?

Make a list of at least five adjectives describing iron.

Can you use this list as starting point for a textile design?

Research

sculpture

book illumination

Knotwork

Take up a notebook and a pen and write the word "knot" in the middle. Then think about at least three textile techniques which are either based on knots or which could be used to integrate knotwork into a quilt or other textile piece. Write them down in the shape of mindmap.

Keep an open view and consider different aspects of piecing, appliqué, embroidery, lacework, etc. Do a little research into lesser known techniques or techniques which aren't practiced so much today (e. g. Macramé). For each technique, add 2 - 3 branches with ideas how to use them in a quilt design. Join techniques with a line if you can imagine combining them in one piece.

Which option is the most interesting?

The Picts

Celtic maze

Selection

What influence has Celtic Art had on subsequent eras of art, craft and design?

"Celtic Revival"

Migrations

The celts were great storytellers and they had indeed lots of stories to tell! After all, they wandered through Europe over the centuries, fighting the Romans and in the end, retreating to the British Isles.

In what ways could such a migration be translated into fabric? What shapes and symbols would you use to tell their stories? Which techniques lend themselves to storytelling in fabric? Look for examples in the quilting world, or even before that, in the history of art and craft.

Would you use different shapes and symbols for the migratory movements of our world today?

Design

Learn more online:

en.wikipedia.org/wiki/Celtic_art

www.bbc.co.uk/wales/celts/factfile/art.shtml

www.britishmuseum.org/explore/highlights/articles/e/early_celtic_or_la_t%C3%A8ne_art.aspx

Real Places to Visit:

National Museum of Scotland, Edinburgh, UK

Museum Manching, Germany

Keltenmuseum Hallein, Austria

Bibracte, Morvan, France

Coincidence Quilt Project - Part 10

How is your Celtic Art project going? Here's another fun distraction...

The tenth part of the Coincidence Quilt Project will tell you how to quilt your Coincidence Quilt Project!

If you have missed the background information for the Coincidence Quilt, please go back to pages 8 and 15.

First and only Level

1   Handquilt your Coincidence Quilt, but don't use any shop-bought stencils.

2   Free-motion quilt your Coincidence Quilt, taking up at least one of the elements you have used before.

3   Join the three layers of your Coincidence Quilt with knots. Space the knots carefully to support your overall design.

4   Use traditional feather motifs in your quilting. You are of course free to interpret these classical patterns as you like.

5   Choose a different focus for your quilting design than for your overall quilt design.

6   Joker: Choose from 1, 2, 3, 4, or 5.

This is the final part of this Coincidence Quilt Project series. You now have all the "ingredients" to design and make your own Coincidence Quilt. Please keep us up to date with your progress and send us pictures of your design, your work in progress and, of course, of your final piece!

If you have questions, contact us at info@quilt-around-the-world.com. We are always happy to help!

In the next chapter, we will start another quilt project relying on the help of our good "friend", the coincidence! Be prepared for another exciting journey!

Coincidence is necessity shrouded in veils.

Marie von Ebner-Eschenbach

Mystery Block Quilt - Part 10

Have you already reached the final stages of your Celtic Art project? No matter how far you have progressed, take a break and enjoy another round of the Mystery Block Quilt.

If you have missed the background information for the Mystery Block Quilt, please go back to pages 8 and 16.

You will find the solution to this block riddle on page 76.

Here are the instructions based on a block designed for you by the Quilt around the World team:

1. The defining elements of this block are two diagonal lines.

2. In addition to the two diagonals, there are 12 identical squares set on point.

3. Moreover, you have to include four identical triangles.

4. We would suggest to use at least 3 different fabrics.

5. The total number of pieces is 40.

> I believe the right question to ask, respecting all ornament, is simply this; was it done with enjoyment, was the carver happy while he was about it?
>
> John Ruskin

This is the solution to the block mystery on page 64.

It is called "Lost Ship" and was first published in 1929.

Detailed patterns for all Mystery Blocks of this series are available on the exhibition catalogue CD which was produced for the My Year of Design TWO travelling exhibition. For ordering information, please go to the Appendix (page 132) or to our website:

www.quilt-around-the-world.com

cubism

Get in the Mood - Cubes

Find a picture or a photo and translate it into a design consisting entirely of squares and rectangles. Either use the blank rectangle on this page or a new page in your sketchbook.

Choose a photo which offers enough variety in form and structure to make this a challenging experience.

Which techniques could you then use to translate your design into fabric?

For EQ7 users: Consider using the Patch Draw Motif feature and upload your photo to the "Transfer image" area.

If you'd like more guidance, please e-mail us at

info@quilt-around-the-world.com

Shape is defined as an enclosed area on a two-dimensional surface. A shape can be created by a curved or bent line which goes back to its point of origin. It can also appear in an arrangement of points or (short) lines. Shapes emerge from their background because of a light-dark contrast, their colour or their texture.

The most commonly used shapes in patchwork are the square, the rectangle, the triangle and the circle.

Dig Deeper – Cubism

Association

early 20th century

Paris

Cézanne

Cubism developed at the beginning of the 20th century and is said to have been strongly influenced by Paul Cézanne's later work.

Braques

avant-garde   **Picasso**

Cubist pioneers were Georges Braques and Pablo Picasso who were later joined by Jean Metzinger, Albert Gleizes, Robert Delaunay, Henri le Fauconnier, Fernand Léger, Juan Gris and others.

Which design aspects, style principles, motifs and objects typical of Cubism do you like best?

multiple viewpoints

cube

simplification

disregard of realism

Cubist artwork objects are analysed, broken up and reassembled in an abstract form. Viewpoints are multiplied which focuses more attention on the subject.

collage

Cubist Sewing Room Waste

Make a "cubist" collage using whatever you find in your sewing room waste. Allow yourself a broad approach and look for fabric scraps, thread "nests", empty spools, waste from foundation piecing projects etc....

Choose an old picture frame, a small wooden tray or a sheet of strong cardboard and place all the objects on this surface. Make sure that you create at least one axis which invites the eye to travel.

Once you are satisfied with the arrangement of your objects, glue them in place (be VERY careful with any sharp or pointed object!). You could use acrylic paint or whatever other paints you have at your disposal to add a few colour accents to your creation.

Could this be the basis for a textile design as well?

Questions

What are the major historic, social and spiritual developments of the Cubist era?

Research

relative motion

simultaneity

Get Movin!

One of the most difficult aspects to express in a picture is movement.

Have you found anything in your research into Cubism which might trick the viewer into a perception of movement? Which shapes, colours, materials could you use?

Section d'Or

Cubist Sculpture

Selection

Cubism and Architecture

Cubist Self

Study one or two Cubist paintings depicting human beings. Look closely and concentrate on the faces. In what way does the artist portray the person(s)?

Then think about ways to create a self-portrait from individual geometric shapes. In what way could you convert these shapes into individual miniature quilts or quilt blocks and combine them into a Cubist fabric self-portrait?

Remember that Cubism is not that interested in depicting nature and that you are supposed to use different viewpoints within the same work. So consider "looking" at yourself from different angles, perhaps also from inside.

Abstract Art

Orphism

Purism

What influence has Cubist Art had on subsequent eras of art, craft and design?

Design

Learn more online:

wikipedia.org/wiki/Cubism

www.metmuseum.org/toah/hd/cube/hd_cube.htm

www.tate.org.uk/learn/online-resources/glossary/c/cubism

www.moma.org/learn/moma_learning/themes/cubism

Real Places to Visit:

Galerie Kubista, Prague, Czech Republic

Centre Pompidou, Paris, France

Museo Nacional Centro de Arte Reina Sofia, Madrid, Spain

Metropolitan Museum of Art, New York, USA

The Tate, London, UK

Coincidental Connections - Round 1

The idea behind Coincidental Connections is to create a wall hanging consisting of eight equal rectangular "blocks" as shown in this diagram.

Each block is 18 units wide (e. g. 18" with one unit being 1", 36 cm with one unit being 2 cm, 45 cm with one unit being 2.5 cm etc.) and 6 units high.

The starting points (referred to as marks) of the lines defining the basic design of the blocks are determined each time by rolling the dice - three times for the next horizontal block side and once for each vertical block side.

Example: Your dice gives you 6 - 4 - 3 for the horizontal block edge. Begin at the left corner and count 6 units towards the right edge. Make a mark. Then continue to count 4 units and make another mark.

Having determined the starting points of the lines, you can then join these marks based on the theme of the round also determined by rolling the dice.

The 1st Round

Upper horizontal edge: .... - .... - ....

Lower horizontal edge: .... - .... - ....

Left-hand side: ....

Right-hand side: ....

Roll the dice once more for the Round 1 theme which will tell you in what way to connect the marks determined above:

1. Use only straight lines to connect marks on opposite block sides.

2. Use at least one curved line to connect marks on adjacent block sides.

3. Add at least one diagonal line to connect marks on adjacent block sides.

4. Connect the marks so that no line is intersecting another line.

5. Connect the marks so that there are as many intersections as possible.

6. Joker - Choose from 1, 2, 3, 4, or 5.

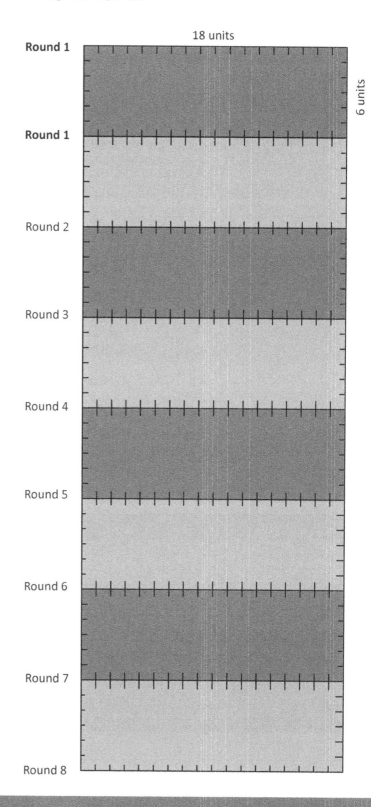

18 units

6 units

Round 1
Round 1
Round 2
Round 3
Round 4
Round 5
Round 6
Round 7
Round 8

You are lost the moment you know what the result will be.

Juan Gris

Mystery Block Quilt - Part 11

Let us drag you away from your Cubist portfolio and do some riddling what is behind the 11th Mystery Block.

If you have missed the background information on the Mystery Block Quilt, please go back to pages 8 and 16.

You will find the solution to this block riddle on page 82.

Here are the instructions based on a traditional block:

1. The block consists of 20 pieces.

2. Although the block doesn't even have triangles, it is still not easy to make.

3. There are only two different shapes.

4. Colour placement will have a strong influence on what you see.

5. Cubist artists would probably have found some affinity with this block.

> Cubism is like standing at a certain point on a mountain and looking around.
> If you go higher, things will look different; if you go lower, again they will look different.
> It is a point of view.
>
> Jacques Lipchitz

This is the solution to the block mystery on page 70.

It is called "Guédelon" and was designed by the Quilt around the World team.

Detailed patterns for all Mystery Blocks of this series are available on the exhibition catalogue CD which was produced for the My Year of Design TWO travelling exhibition. For ordering information, please go to the Appendix (page 132) or to our website:

www.quilt-around-the-world.com

Baroque

Get in the Mood - Circular Composition

This painting by Peter Paul Rubens is based on an intriguing circular composition. We have included a diagram to demonstrate this. Can you see it in Rubens' picture?

Take this circular composition and use it to design a block or a small quilt. Which techniques best suit such a piece?

Peter Paul Rubens
The rape of the daughters of Leucippos (ca. 1618)

My talent is such that no undertaking, however vast in size... has ever surpassed my courage.

Peter Paul Rubens

Dig Deeper - Baroque

Association

"irregularly shaped pearl"

17th century

What are the major historic, social and spiritual developments of the Baroque era?

The Baroque started around 1600 in Italy and quickly spread to most of Europe.

"life is a dream"   emotions

Rococo

Don Quijote

Baroque is often associated with exaggeration, drama, tension, exuberance and grandeur in all aspects of art.

Vermeer   **Caravaggio**

Velázquez

Which design aspects, style principles, motifs and objects typical of Baroque art do you like best?

oval

chiaroscuro   ## Questions

Like a Fleeting Dream

Sonnets are poems of fourteen lines which follow a strict rhyme scheme. The first sonnets ever written date back to the 13th century. Important themes in Baroque sonnets were "Carpe diem" (Enjoy the day), "Memento mori" (remember that you will die eventually) and "Vanitas" (vanity). In the following, we have included three lines from the sonnet "All is Vanity" by Andreas Gryphius (1616 - 1664) which evidently belongs to the "Vanitas" theme:

There is nothing which is eternal, no metal, no marble stone.

Now Fortune smiles on us, but soon hardships will threaten

The fame of great deeds must be like a fleeting dream.

Do these beautiful lines inspire you enough to translate them into fabric? Do Andreas Gryphius's lines have some implications for our modern times?

Research

jesuits

power

What do you find most interesting about Baroque art and its artists?

Power Gardens

During the Baroque era, not only the so-called fine arts developed their own and very particular style. The craving to express power and wealth extended to architecture - palaces were built, re-built or extended and so were the gardens belonging to the palaces. And not only as an afterthought, but as an important part of the overall design and concept.

Originating in the Italian Renaissance gardens, the quintessential Baroque gardens were established in France which is why this garden style is often referred to as "French Garden". The most famous example certainly is the Versailles garden as shown on the map by Delagrife (1746).

When you think about such a Baroque garden, with its symmetry and strong formalism, can you think of a quilt block or a small quilt imitating this structure?

Plan of Versailles - palace and gardens Delagrife (1746)

The Baroque style was favoured not solely by the aristocracy who saw the style as a way to impress others and to express triumph, power and control. Baroque art was also encouraged by the Catholic Church which, to counter-balance the influence of the Protestant Reformation, used art as a means of communicating religious themes emphasizing direct and emotional involvement.

Selection

Light and Shadow

Caravaggio (1571 - 1610), another eminent Baroque painter, is considered the master of "chiaroscuro" meaning the use of light and shadow to create three-dimensionality on a flat canvas.

In what way can traditional patchwork blocks be changed by varying the colour values (light, medium, dark)? Look for block examples and experiment with different colour placements. How simple or complicated must/can a block be to create a 3D effect? What role do patterns play in this context?

Design

Learn more online:

en.wikipedia.org/wiki/Baroque

www.britannica.com/art/Baroque-period

www.visual-arts-cork.com/history-of-art/baroque.htm

www.metmuseum.org/toah/hd/baro/hd_baro.htm

Real Places to Visit:

Museo Nacional del Prado, Madrid, Spain

Rubenshuis, Antwerpen, Netherlands

Alte Pinakothek, München, Germany

Wieskirche, Steingaden, Germany

Coincidental Connections - Round 2

At the habitual place, we have some distraction for you. And therefore it is again time to get out the dice and work on the 2nd round of Coincidental Connections.

If you have missed the background information on Coincidental Connections, please go back to page 75.

The 2ⁿᵈ Round

Horizontal: .... - .... - ....

Left-hand side: ....

Right-hand side: ....

Roll the dice once more for the Round 2 block theme:

1. Include at least one "S" shaped line when connecting your marks.

2. Include at least one "Z" shaped line when connecting your marks.

3. Connect two lines with another line forming an "H".

4. Draw another line starting at one of the marks at the top of your block and finishing at a different mark from the line you previously drew.

5. Connect two lines with another line forming an "F".

6. Joker - Choose from 1, 2, 3, 4, or 5.

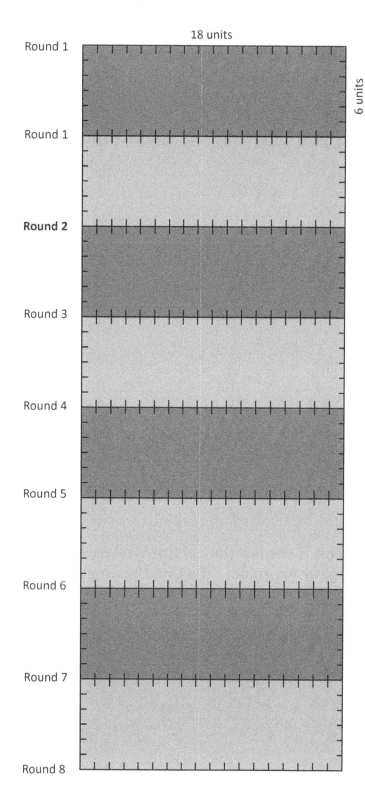

18 units

6 units

Round 1
Round 1
Round 2
Round 3
Round 4
Round 5
Round 6
Round 7
Round 8

There is only one valuable thing in art: the thing you cannot explain.

Georges Braques

Mystery Block Quilt - Part 12

At the end of your Baroque project, we have a little diversion for you - the 12th part of the Mystery Block Quilt.

If you have missed the background information on the Mystery Block Quilt please go back to pages 8 and 16.

You will find the solution to this block riddle on page 88.

Here are the instructions based on a block designed for you by the Quilt around the World team:

1. The block is rather complicated with a total of three different sub-units.

2. The first sub-unit is simple and consists of four identical pieces. This sub-unit is used the least of all sub-units.

3. The second sub-unit consists of five pieces and there is at least one square, one rectangle and one other shape.

4. The third sub-unit would best be sewn using Foundation Piecing and could be interpreted as stylized sun rays.

5. You should use all colour values (light, medium, dark) and at least five different fabrics.

This is the last part of the Mystery Block Quilt project. On page 88, we are starting a new mystery project - the Line Drawing Mystery Project.

In order to attain the impossible, one must attempt the absurd.

Miguel de Cervantes

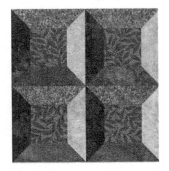

This is the solution to the block mystery on page 76.

It is called "Lattice Square" which has been around for many, many years.

Detailed patterns for all Mystery Blocks of this series are available on the exhibition catalogue CD which was produced for the My Year of Design TWO travelling exhibition. For ordering informa-tion, please go to the Appendix (page 132) or to our website:

www.quilt-around-the-world.com

Aboriginal Art

Get in the Mood - Dreaming

We Westerners cannot begin to understand the nature and meaning of the Aboriginal "Dreaming". For them, it defines the spiritual, natural and ethical order of the cosmos. "Dreamtime" begins in the times before the creation of the universe and ends before human memory. It does not refer to dreaming in your sleep and is not considered unreal. It is a state of truth beyond earthly reality.

Dreaming tells the stories of the supernatural ancestors, e. g. the rainbow serpent, the ghosts of lightning, the Wagilag sisters, the Tingari and the Wandjina who created everything and laid down the laws for social and religious behaviour.

Imagine that our (western) culture also had a Dreaming. What would be important? What would our supernatural ancestors look like? Would there also be a rainbow serpent? Which customs and rituals would express our Dreaming?

Use the empty space here or a new page in your sketchbook for a few sketches of your own Dreaming. What would a textile piece based on this look like?

We are near waking
when we dream we are dreaming.

Novalis

Dig Deeper - Aboriginal Art

Association

dot painting

What do you find most interesting about Aboriginal art?

Aboriginal art is one of the oldest continuous art traditions in the world and dates back over 50,000 years and is very much alive and thriving in the 21st century.

painting on leaves

yellow, brown, red, white

rock carving

Aboriginal art appears in the form of rock carvings, rock paintings, body painting, painting on bark and leaves, wood sculpture, weaving etc.

Which design aspects, style principles, motifs and objects typical of Aboriginal art do you like best?

Mimih

rainbow serpent

The Aboriginal culture does not esteem material possessions, but knowledge. Art is an expression of knowledge and therefore a kind of legitimisation. By using the patterns handed down by their ancestors, artists claim their identity, and also their rights and duties.

tradition

Questions

Dreaming

Dot Paintings

In Aboriginal art, dots play a very important role. They are usually of different paint colours each of which has its own meaning (e. g. yellow representing the sun, brown the soil, red the desert sand etc.). Dot paintings often have a religious background and motivation and frequently depict animals, lakes or the dreamtime.

Where can we find accumulations of dots in our world, no matter whether in the natural or our man-made environment? Is there a meaning behind these dot "paintings"?

Make a design based on one of these dot clusters and create your own colour coding. Make one or two variations of your design. Which do you like best?

In what ways could your design be translated into fabric?

Research

Rainbow Serpent

The Rainbow Serpent is an important element in Aboriginal mythology and plays a signficant role in Dreaming. It appears both as a female forming mountains, valleys and water sources and as a male embodying the sun and therefore creating the rainbow.

Draw a Rainbow Serpent (either in your sketchbook or in the empty space below). What will you focus on, the female or the male form? Or can you create an image encompassing both?

Selection

David Malangi   **Papunya Tula**

Albert Namatjira

What influence has Aboriginal art had and still has on other forms of art, craft and design?

Design

Learn more online:

en.wikipedia.org/wiki/Indigenous_Australian_art

www.australia.gov.au/about-australia/australian-story/austn-indigenous-art

www.kateowengallery.com/page/10-Facts-About-Aboriginal-Art.aspx

Real Places to Visit:

National Museum of Australia, Canberra, Australia

Museum voor hedendaagse Aboriginal kunst, Utrecht, Netherlands

British Museum, London, UK

Museum Fünf Kontinente, München, Germany

Coincidental Connections - Round 3

As usual, we are asking our good friend, the coincidence, to assist us in the 3rd round of Coincidental Connections.

If you have missed the background information for the Coincidental Connections, please go back to page 75.

The 3ʳᵈ Round

Horizontal: .... - .... - ....

Left-hand side: ....

Right-hand side: ....

Roll the dice once more for the Round 3 Block theme:

1. Repeat what you did for Round 1.

2. Choose an option from Round 1 which you haven't used yet.

3. Repeat what you did for Round 2.

4. Choose an option from Round 2 which you haven't used yet.

5. Combine what you did for Round 1 and for Round 2.

6. Joker - Choose from 1, 2, 3, 4, or 5.

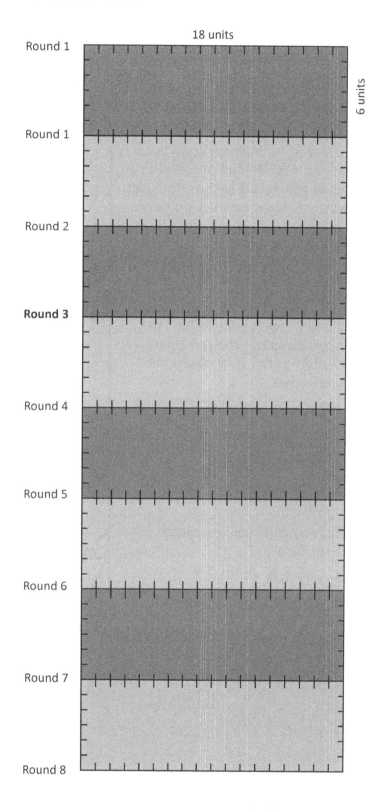

18 units

6 units

Round 1
Round 1
Round 2
Round 3
Round 4
Round 5
Round 6
Round 7
Round 8

A coincidence is an unforeseen event which makes sense.

Diogenes

Line Drawing Mystery - Part 1

The Line Drawing Mystery is just that - a line drawing of a mysterious motif chopped into 6 pieces with only a minimum of information on colour values and textures.

The goal of this exercise and its 5 sequels is to send you on a creative journey without a planned and known outcome. An expedition into unknown design lands, so to speak. **The objective is not to get as close as possible to the underlying motif at record speed!**

Use the line drawing shown to create a block. The size of the block is up to you as well as the techniques you use. Make a monochrome project or use boldly colourful fabrics. Add embellishments as you go or wait for the unveiling of the complete picture.

The orientation shown is not necessarily the orientation from the original picture. The Line Drawing Mystery parts will appear in random order.

A few hints on Part 1:

1   Lightest areas

2   Slightly darker than 1

3 - 6   Smooth surface, becoming darker

7   fairly dark, neither smooth nor uniform

8   very dark

9   dark lines, smooth and light surfaces

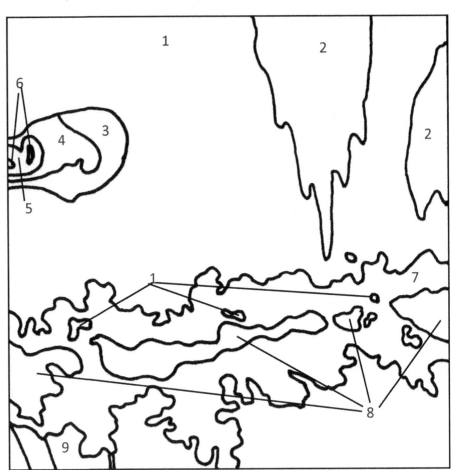

Where there is mystery,
it is generally suspected that there must also be evil.

Lord Byron

This is the solution to the block mystery on page 82.

It is called "Grande Finale" and was designed by the Quilt around the World team.

Detailed patterns for all Mystery Blocks of this series are available on the exhibition catalogue CD which was produced for the My Year of Design TWO travelling exhibition. For ordering information, please go to the Appendix (page 132) or to our website:

www.quilt-around-the-world.com

Art Nouveau

Get in the Mood - Line Patterns

Curved lines play an important role in Art Nouveau. They show floral shapes and the most extreme forms have even been called "whiplash" lines.

We have created the beginning of a pattern based on such a "whiplash". Use it as a basis for a more elaborate pattern in your own style.

Patterns consist of repeated, modified, alternating, symmetrical or asymmetrical shapes which have a close relationship with each other. Whenever a group of motifs is repeated, it is called a repeat or rapport.

Patterns follow a rhythm which can be regular, irregular or varied.

Within a pattern, the size relationship between elements is important especially taking into consideration the object the pattern might ultimately cover. In general, large-scale patterns will be more suitable for larger objects while smaller objects would demand small-scale patterns.

Dig Deeper - Art Nouveau

Association

Paris Métro

floral shapes

Art Nouveau was most popular from 1890 until 1910.

Which design aspects, style principles, motifs and objects typical of Art Nouveau do you like best (or least)?

whiplash

Japanese influence

Art Nouveau is inspired by natural forms and structures, flowers and plants and curved lines in general.

What do you find most interesting about Art Nouveau and its creations? Which artist do you consider most intriguing?

Tiffany

Klimt

Gaudì

Mackintosh

Mucha

Loïe Fuller

Questions

typograhpy

new materials

New in Town...

The Art Nouveau artists were keen to use the "new" materials such as concrete, only recently available.

Choose one material yourself which you have never worked with before. Take a broad approach and consider non-textiles as well as found objects, items from a hardware store or a garden centre, a stationers, a pharmacy etc.

Explore its possibilities and limitations and create a small block or quilt.

Is there a particular design aspect which you can achieve with this material and which you couldn't create with the materials you have used previously? Will you use it again?

Research

Art Nouveau influenced many art forms, such as architecture, graphic art, interior design, most of the decorative arts including jewellery, furniture, textiles, plus the fine arts.

A Glimpse Beneath the Surface

Both Antoní Gaudí and Frank Lloyd Wright are considered by some art historians not really to belong to the Art Nouveau as they seem to form their very own architectural "category". Yet, these two fascinating gentlemen offer some parallels in their work, notably the dissolution of the outer skin of their buildings with the help of different techniques, materials and designs.

Can you create a textile design where the outer skin, i. e. the top of a quilt, partly "dissolves" to allow the viewer a glimpse of what lies beneath?

Which techniques and materials are suitable for such a project?

Will you choose the vegetal structures so typical for Antonì Gaudí or the more functional and straight lines and planes used by Frank Lloyd Wright?

Secese   **Stile Liberty**   **Modernisme**

Modern Style   international style

Jugendstil

Sezession

Art Deco

Selection

Not Only History Repeats Itself

Art Nouveau quickly lost in popularity after World War I as the materials used were too expensive and people got fed up with the exuberant lines, shapes and ornamentation. Originating in France, Art Deco soon became the new high fashion, combining traditional craft elements with contemporary imagery and materials belonging very much to the Machine Age.

Art Deco is, among others, characterized by strong geometric shapes, such as spheres, polygons, rectangles, trapezoids, zigzags, chevrons, and sunburst motifs often arranged in symmetrical patterns.

Can you create a pattern using as many of these geometrical shapes as possible? Can you create a pattern repeat, i. e. a pattern unit which can be added to itself in all directions to create an all-over pattern?

Design

Learn more online:

en.wikipedia.org/wiki/Art_Nouveau

www.theartstory.org/movement-art-nouveau.htm

www.visual-arts-cork.com/history-of-art/art-nouveau.htm

www.britannica.com/art/Art-Nouveau

Real Places to Visit:

Paris

Vienna

Barcelona

Prague

Munich

Coincidental Connections - Round 4

Again it is time to get out the dice and continue with Coincidental Connections.

If you have missed the background information on the Coincidental Connections, go back to page 75.

The 4ᵗʰ Round

Horizontal: .... - .... - ....

Left-hand side: ....

Right-hand side: ....

Roll the dice once more for the Round 4 Block theme:

1. Join the marks with straight lines using the most direct connection.
2. Join the marks with curved lines using the most direct connection.
3. Join the marks with straight lines and add at least two more lines which connect some of the lines drawn previously.
4. Join the marks with curved lines and add at least two more lines which connect some of the lines drawn previously.
5. Join the marks with the help of quarter, half and three-quarter circles.
6. Joker - Choose from 1, 2, 3, 4, or 5.

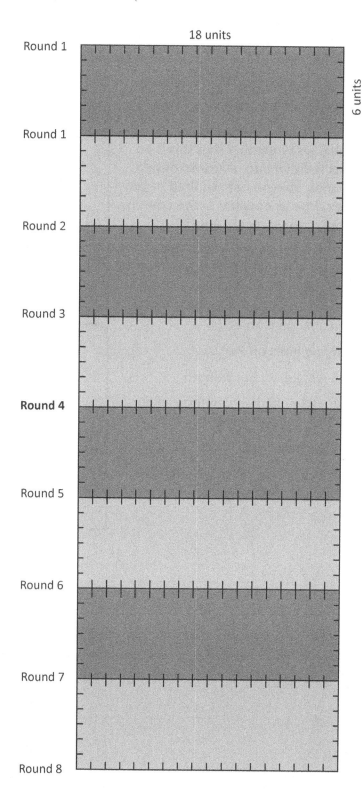

Round 1

18 units

Round 1

6 units

Round 2

Round 3

Round 4

Round 5

Round 6

Round 7

Round 8

Want it and set to work briskly.

Friedrich Schiller

Line Drawing Mystery - Part 2

The Line Drawing Mystery is just that - a line drawing of a mysterious motif chopped into 6 pieces with only a minimum of information on colour values and textures.

Please go back to Part 1 (page 88) for details on this series of exercises.

Always remember that this is an expedition into unknown design lands. You are not required to get as close as possible to the underlying motif at record speed!

The orientation shown is not necessarily the orientation from the original picture. The parts of the Line Drawing Mystery will appear in a random order.

A few hints on Part 2:

1 very dark, not smooth

2 rather dark, no uniform colours, no uniform texture

3 lightest area

4 slightly darker than 3, no clear delimitations

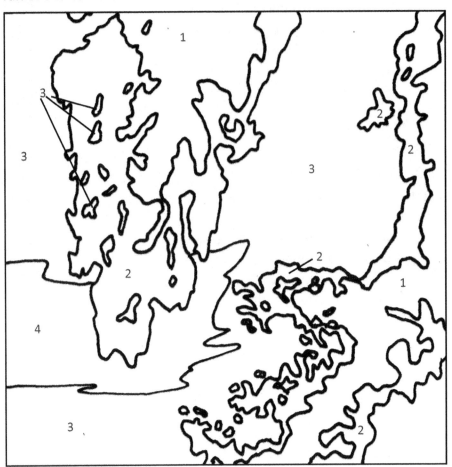

There are no straight lines or sharp corners in nature. Therefore, buildings should have no straight lines or sharp corners.

Antoni Gaudí

If you are wondering what could be behind the Line Mystery:

The major motif is a man-made structure, a very impressive piece of art...

Concrete Art

Get in the Mood - $a^2 + b^2 = c^2$

Concrete Art was first defined in a manifesto written by the artist Theo van Doesburg as not referring to or alluding to elements which can be found in the visible world. Concrete Art accordingly was to be totally abstract and entirely a "brain product".

So why not start the design process with a mathematical equation? Of course we chose the formula best known and well "loved" by quilters - Pythagoras!

Can you create a design based on squares representing this theorem?

Hint

Why don't you produce a design with three squares following this equation? To calculate the sizes of the squares, start with a and b, multiply each with itself, add them together and find the square root of the sum. Round to the next "cuttable" size and start playing!

The horizon of human vision has widened and art has annexed new territories that were formerly denied to it.

Max Bill

If you are interested in learning more about Design Elements, Design Principles and Composition, you might want to consider taking part in "My Year of Design THREE", an online course split into three modules with 6 chapters each.

For more information, please go to the Appendix (page 133) or to our website:

www.quilt-around-the-world.com/MYoD3

Dig Deeper - Concrete Art

Association

geometry

Which design aspects, style principles, motifs and objects typical for Concrete Art do you like best?

In its ideal form, Concrete Art is based on mathematics and geometry.

"directly from the mind"

rhythm

lines, planes, colours

Concrete Art evolved in the 1920s and 1930s and found its theoretical ground-work in Theo van Doesburg's manifesto "The Basis of Concrete Art".

Theo van Doesburg

De Stijl

Questions

Concrete Art is sometimes considered a close relative of "Constructivism".

Black Square

A Quilter's Logo

When reading about Concrete Art, "traditional" quilters especially will at once recognize themselves as Concrete Artists.

So why don't you create your very own logo based on the Concrete Art principles:

- no representation of reality
- no symbolic meaning
- pure geometric construction
- colour as basic substance

Create a block similar to your best-loved "traditional" block or make an entirely new design...

Research

Max Bill

Möbius Strip

Max Bill, one of the most famous Concrete Artists, liked to experiment with the so-called Möbius Strip, a geometric phenomenon first described in the 19th century by the mathematicians August Ferdinand Möbius and Johann Benedict Listing.

A Möbius Strip is a surface with only one side and only one boundary. You can easily make a model of a Möbius Strip by cutting a paper strip and joining its ends AFTER giving the strip a half-twist. This is only one example - there is a wide variety of geometric possibilities for Möbius bands.

Möbius Strips invite us to play with its curious properties, e. g. draw a line down the middle starting at the seam or cut the Möbius Strip along the centre line.

Can you think of ways to integrate a Möbius Strip in your textile work?

art and design

Selection

Piet Mondrian

Mondrian's Legacy

Many will be familiar with Mondrian's later work as the strong geometrics and primary colours of these paintings have been widely used in fashion, advertising, architecture and many other fields.

Look up one or two of these paintings on the Internet (or if possible, go to a museum to look at an original) and contemplate the lines, shapes and colours used.

Then take out your sketchbook and create a design for a quilt block or small quilt using

- at least three thick black lines
- at least one blue, one red and one yellow square or rectangle
- at least one design element NOT used by Mondrian

Make more than one design and put them away for a few days. Then come back to your designs, decide which is your favourite (and why) and translate it into fabric.

What influences has Concrete Art had on other eras of art, craft and design? What are the parallels of Concrete Art and patchwork?

Design

Learn more online:

en.wikipedia.org/wiki/Concrete_art

en.wikipedia.org/wiki/De_Stijl

www.tate.org.uk/learn/online-resources/glossary/c/concrete-art

www.visual-arts-cork.com/definitions/concrete-art.htm

Real Places to Visit:

Museum für Konkrete Kunst Design, Ingolstadt, Germany

Museum Haus Konstruktiv, Zürich, Switzerland

Mondriaanhuis, Amersfoort, Netherlands

Metropolitan Museum of Art, New York, USA

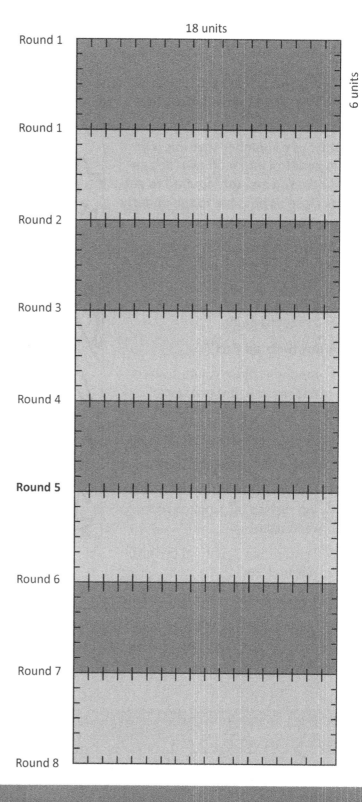

Coincidental Connections - Round 5

If you need a little break from your portfolio work on Concrete Art, why don't you play a little with your dice and with Coincidental Connections?

If you have missed the background information for the Coincidental Connections, go back to page 75.

The 5th Round

Horizontal: .... - .... - ....

Left-hand side: ....

Right-hand side: ....

Roll the dice once more for the Round 5 Block theme:

1. Repeat what you did for round 3.

2. Choose an option from round 3 which you haven't used yet.

3. Repeat what you did for round 4.

4. Choose an option from round 4 which you haven't used yet.

5. Combine what you did for round 3 and for round 4.

6. Joker - Choose from 1, 2, 3, 4, or 5.

18 units

6 units

Round 1
Round 1
Round 2
Round 3
Round 4
Round 5
Round 6
Round 7
Round 8

Whoever says he is starting from a given in nature may be right, and so is he who says he is starting from nothing!

Piet Mondrian

Line Drawing Mystery - Part 3

The Line Drawing Mystery is just that - a line drawing of a mysterious motif chopped into 6 pieces with only a minimum of information on colour values and textures.

Please go back to Part 1 (page 88) for details on this series of exercises.

Always remember that this is an expedition into unknown design lands. You are not required to get as close as possible to the underlying motif at record speed!

The orientation shown is not necessarily the orientation from the original picture. The parts of the Line Drawing Mystery will appear in a random order.

A few hints on Part 3:

1 medium colour value, surface not smooth, but not rough either

2 darker than 1, natural texture

3 very dark, surface not smooth

4 man-made smooth and reflecting surface (all squares and rectangles)

5 lighter than 3, natural texture, not uniform

6 man-made surface, fairly smooth

Remember:
You can always adapt MYoD exercises if your design process makes this desirable. While we would encourage you to take up the challenges we present to you, at the same time it's up to you whether you reduce and simplify!

If you are wondering what could be behind this Line Mystery:

You can find it out of doors and in Central Europe...

Precolumbian Art

Get in the Mood - Go for Gold

Gold was the most important metal for the Incas. Their sun god Inti was believed to be embodied in gold and some Inca buildings in their capital were literally covered with it.

Here, we have prepared a very basic pattern for you which could be anything - an appliqué or even reverse appliqué motif, an embroidery or tapestry pattern etc.

Take up this pattern and - with the help of gold - add a secondary or even a tertiary pattern lending some Inca glamour to the simple rhythm of the pattern.

In what ways could your sketch be translated into a textile piece? Which techniques and which materials could be used? Would you consider using non-textile elements in your final piece?

Everything has its limit -
iron ore cannot be educated into gold.

Mark Twain

Dig Deeper - Precolumbian Art

Association

Christopher Columbus

The term "Precolumbian Art" encompasses the visual arts of indigenous people of the Caribbean, North, Central, and South Americas until the late 15th and early 16th century.

What do you find most interesting about Precolumbian Art?

The oldest artefacts date back to 13,000 BCE.

Inca

Maya

Olmecs

Paracas

Toltecs   Aztecs

Chavin

Moche

What are the major historic, social and spiritual developments of the different Precolumbian Cultures?

rock paintings

sculpture

ceramics

Questions

textiles

Mysterious Ancient Lines

As you know, we like mysteries very much. My Year of Design brings you many mysteries and riddles to play with. This is no surprise as our beautiful world is full of mysteries.

Among the most fascinating mysteries of mankind are the Nazca Lines located in the Nazca desert in southern Peru. These geoglyphs were designated as a UNESCO Cultural Heritage Site in 1994. Although their origins are still disputed by the experts, they are mostly attributed to the Nazca Culture (500 BCE - 500 CE). Nazca Lines range from simple lines to stylized motifs, mostly drawn from nature.

For this exercise, choose your favourite bird and draw it using only one line - complete with beak, head, wings, feathers, tail and feet. If you like, reduce reality to the "essence" of your motif.

What could you do with your single line drawing? In what ways could you translate it into a quilt block or small quilt?

Research

As many of the precolumbian cultures didn't have writing systems, visual art expressed cosmologies, world views, religion and philosophy and sometimes also served as a mnenomic system.

A Quilt is not a Relief, but...

A relief in art is a sculptural technique where sculpted elements remain attached to a background of the same material. This is also true for a quilt. However, sculpture usually involves taking away material while quilting compresses the material in some areas which makes others stand out - just as in sculpted reliefs.

Maya art shows many images in relief and many surfaces are decorated in this way.

For this exercise, find typical Maya patterns (or create of your own) and create a quilted "relief" by dense quilting (hand or machine) or seed stitching. Unless you have plenty of time, choose a small format for hand quilting/stitching.

What techniques could further enhance the relief-like surface of your piece?

Selection

Your Colossal Self

The Olmec people created sculptures of colossal heads, presumably depicting important leaders. The earlier heads are especially realistic and unidealised portrayals of the men.

We are not going to ask you to make a colossal head, but we would like you to design a self-portrait (again), this time concentrating on the shadows sculpting your features. It is not necessary to create a perfect liking, just concentrate on the darker areas of your face, on the shades cast by your nose and your mouth, perhaps on some lines past experience has left on your face etc.

If you like, experiment with different light settings. What happens if parts of your face are thrown into the dark?

In what ways could you translate your sketch into fabric? Which techniques are most suitable to project your self-portrait onto fabric? Also consider colour manipulation to recreate your sketch!

Design

Learn more online:

en.wikipedia.org/wiki/Pre-Columbian_art

www.encyclopedia.com/topic/pre-Columbian_art_and_architecture.aspx

www.metmuseum.org/visit/museum-map/galleries/africa-oceania-and-the-americas/357

mayaincaaztec.com/inarthi.html

Real Places to Visit:

Museo del Arte Precolombino, Cusco, Peru

Museo de América, Madrid, Spain

Museo Chileno de Arte Precolombino, Santiago, Chile

Rijksmuseum Volkenkunde, Leiden, Netherlands

Amercian Museum of Natural History, New York, USA

Coincidental Connections - Round 6

Again you will need your dice to find out what the 6th round has in store for your Coincidental Connections.

If you have missed the background information for the Coincidental Connections, please go back to page 75.

The 6ᵗʰ Round

Horizontal: .... - .... - ....

Left-hand side: ....

Right-hand side: ....

Roll the dice once more for the Round 6 Block theme:

1. Join the marks with straight lines and include medium sized circles in these lines

2. Join the marks with curved lines and insert medium sized squares in these lines.

3. Join the marks with straight lines and add at least one more line - a vertical line starting at a mark from the very first horizontal line, going through one of the marks from this round and ending at the very last horizontal line. If this is not possible, choose marks from round 1 and this round which are closest together relative to a vertical line and draw a vertical line between them from top to bottom.

4. Join the marks with curved lines and add at least one more curved line which connects a mark from the first round with one mark from this round and going through the very last horizontal line.

5. Join the marks with the help of quarter, half and three-quarter circles.

6. Joker - Choose from 1, 2, 3, 4, or 5.

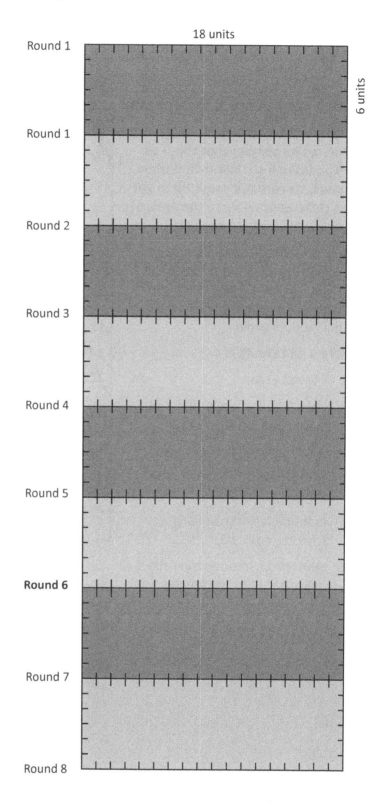

18 units

6 units

Round 1
Round 1
Round 2
Round 3
Round 4
Round 5
Round 6
Round 7
Round 8

If coincidende mixes the card,
the brain loses the game.

German proverb

Line Drawing Mystery - Part 4

The Line Drawing Mystery is just that - a line drawing of a mysterious motif hacked into 6 pieces with only a minimum of information on colour values and textures.

Please go back to Part 1 (see page 88) for details on this series of exercises.

Always remember that this is an expedition into unknown design lands. You are not required to get as close as possible to the underlying motif at record speed!

The orientation shown is not necessarily the orientation from the original picture. The parts of the Line Drawing Mystery will appear in a random order.

A few hints on Part 4:

1 lightest area

2 very dark, surface not smooth

3 lighter than 2, natural texture, not uniform

4 lighter than 3, otherwise the same

5 man-made surface, fairly smooth, not dark

6 man-made smooth and reflecting surface (all "rectangles")

7 Smooth surface, different shades of the same colour

God as you tell me,
was put to death by the very men He created.
But my God still looks down on His children.

Atahualpa, Inca Chief

If you are wondering what could be behind this Line Mystery:

While the artwork can be found in Europe, the maker is an US-American...

Ancient Greece

Get in the Mood - Shadow Play

One of the most famous works in Ancient Greek philosophy is the Allegory of the Cave narrated by the philosopher Plato (ca. 428/427 - 348/347 BC) as a dialogue between his teacher Socrates and his brother Glaucon.

The Allegory of the Cave describes a group of prisoners who have lived all their lives chained to a wall without ever seeing daylight. They watch shadows of forms projected onto this wall and they start naming them.

Look around you. Can you see any interesting shadows in your surroundings? Concentrate on the shadow shapes and consider their essence. Try to forget the object which casts the shadow and let your imagination run riot with what else could be hidden here.

Make a sketch and translate your design into fabric.

The beginning is the most important part of the work.

Plato

Dig Deeper - Ancient Greece

Association

Olympus

Mythology

Venus

Historians divide Ancient Greek Art into four major periods of different styles: the Geometric, the Archaic, the Classical and the Hellenistic Eras.

Parthenon

Plato

Aristotle

Epicurus

Alexander the Great

Which design aspects, style principles, motifs and objects typical for Ancient Greek Art do you like best?

Our view on Ancient Greek Art is largely based on what was best conserved over the millenia, i. e. architecture, sculpture, pottery and some painting, however it is to be assumed that the Ancient Greeks practiced all art forms.

pottery

sculpture

coins

Questions

mosaics

Pergamon Altar

polychromy

What are the major historic, social and spiritual developments of the Ancient Greek Art era?

Red on Black

The Ancient Greeks were proficient potters and made many vessels mostly for everyday use. Historians distinguish many different phases of both patterns and colouring.

For this exercise, we will concentrate on the red-figure technique. Here, pots were painted black and all added motifs were kept in red.

Take up this reduced colour scheme and make two or three designs for a textile piece based on a black background and one or more red motifs. Think broadly both as to subject matter and technique(s).

Put your designs aside for a few days. Then take them up again and decide which design is your favourite. If necessary, continue to work on the design and make plans how to translate it into fabric.

Research

Colour Splurge

Although most of us have an image of white sculptures and white buildings against an irrisistibly blue sky when asked about (Ancient) Greece, historians tell us that this conception is false. Both the sculptures and a large part of Ancient Greek architecture were painted in a multitude of colours.

Do the same - choose a block, either "traditional" or "contemporary", and use as many different colours as possible. Make a sketch first and go wild with your coloured pencils! Don't think about colour theory - just splurge on with your paintbox and don't give a thought to whether the colours match or follow any kind of predefined scheme.

Put away your sketch for a few days. Then take it up again and consider your design. Perhaps you might also want to pin it up a wall and look at it from a distance. Is there anything you particularly like about your colour splurge? Or is there anything you would like to change?

When you are satisfied, think of ways to put your block into fabrics. Will you use only solids or add additional complexity by different patterns?

Selection

Prime Blocks

Prime numbers are numbers greater than 1 that have no positive divisors other than 1 and themselves. The first ten prime numbers are:

2, 3, 5, 7, 11, 13, 17, 19, 23, 29

When a number doesn't have a divisor, this means that it is quite difficult to set this number of blocks into a quilt. For this exercise, we ask you to play with the numbers above and think of quilt layouts for each prime number.

If you like, choose your favourite layout and include block sketches, different sashing options etc.

Ancient Greek Art has widely influenced the art and culture of many countries all over the world, especially in sculpture and architecture.

Design

Learn more online:

en.wikipedia.org/wiki/Ancient_Greek_art
www.history.com/topics/ancient-history/ancient-greek-art
ancient-greece.org/art.html
www.metmuseum.org/toah/hd/tacg/hd_tacg.htm

Real Places to Visit:

Acropolis, Athens, Greece
National Archaeological Museum, Athens, Greece
Altes Museum, Berlin, Germany
British Museum, London, UK
Museum of Fine Arts, Boston, USA

© Quilt around the World

Coincidental Connections - Round 7

At the usual place we have prepared the next round of Coincidental Connections. Take out your dice and see what round 7 will bring.

If you have missed the background information for Coincidental Connections, please go to page 75.

The 7th Round

Horizontal: .... - .... - ....

Left-hand side: ....

Right-hand side: ....

Roll the dice once more for the Round 7 Block theme:

1. Repeat what you did for round 6.

2. Choose an option from round 6 which you haven't used yet.

3. Combine what you did for round 6 and for round 1.

4. Combine what you did for round 6 and for round 2.

5. Combine what you did for round 6 and for round 4.

6. Joker - Choose from 1, 2, 3, 4, or 5.

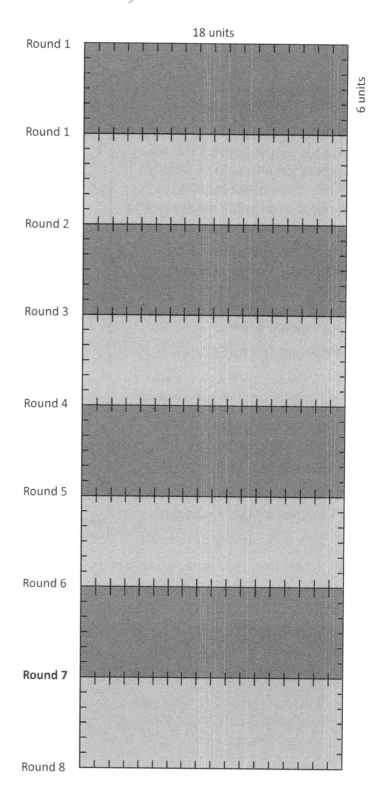

Round 1
Round 1
Round 2
Round 3
Round 4
Round 5
Round 6
Round 7
Round 8

18 units

6 units

There is no great genius without some touch of madness.

Aristotle

Line Drawing Mystery - Part 5

The Line Drawing Mystery is just that - a line drawing of a mysterious motif chopped into 6 pieces with only a minimum of information on colour values and textures.

Please go back to Part 1 (page 88) for details on this series of exercises.

Always remember that this is an expedition into unknown design lands. You are not required to get as close as possible to the underlying motif at record speed!

The orientation shown is not necessarily the orientation from the original picture. The parts of the Line Drawing Mystery will appear in a random order.

A few hints on Part 5:

1 - 3 Smooth surface, different shades of the same colour

4 man-made surface, medium dark, fairly smooth

5 natural texture, not smooth

6 man-made smooth and reflecting surface (all "rectangles")

7 very dark, surface not smooth

8 lighter than 7, natural texture, not uniform

9 man-made surface, fairly smooth, not dark

I have never wished to cater to the crowd; for what I know they do not approve, and what they approve, I do not know.

Epicurus

If you are wondering what could be behind this Line Mystery:

The place is easily accessible...

Architecture

Get in the Mood - The Fabric of a Building

Think about buildings you like - in your vicinity, in your town, your country or on the entire planet. Why do you like them? Do they have something in common? Are they old or new, by well-known architects or just "normal" houses?

Choose one of these buildings and think about its defining elements. Decide on one or two of these elements and use them as basis for a design. Use the space on this page or a blank page of your sketchbook.

Put away your design for a few days. Then take it up again, decide whether you'd like to change it and then translate it into a textile piece.

What would happen if you chose a building which you didn't like?

We shape our buildings;
thereafter they shape us.

Winston Churchill

Dig Deeper - Architecture

Association

planning, designing and constructing

bridges

cities

houses

gardens

Architecture is the planning and constructing of structures to define and confine space to reflect functional, technical, social, environmental and aesthetical requirements.

Ornamentation

For millenia, ornamentation has played an important role in architecture. Many buildings carry rich ornamentation on their outside and inside walls to please the eye of the viewer, to show wealth and power, to document affiliation with a social group etc.

Find an ornamented building in your vicinity and use the shapes (and colours if applicable) for a design. Will you use the ornamentation as it is or will you adapt it to create something entirely new?

Questions

In what ways does architecture shape our lives? In what ways does it represent what mankind has thought and believed?

Facades

A facade is an outside and visible "skin" of a building, usually the front. Very often, the facade represents the overall design of the building.

Look at different types of facades in buildings around you. Consider doing some research online or consult books on architecture.

Select one example which you find most interesting. Analyse its components and decide on one aspect which you could use in a textile piece.

Research

Le Corbusier

Brunelleschi

Eiffel

Wren

Calatrava

Sullivan

Gaudì

Palladio

Lloyd Wright

Niemeyer

Which architect do you like best? Has your research influenced your likes and dislikes?

Selection

Settlements

Think about the town or village you live in and what it looks like from above. Don't use a map, just your own imagination.

Draw lines for the most important streets and add squares and rectangles for the buildings. Then use colours to distinguish areas you like and areas you dislike.

Can you use this sketch as basis for a textile piece?

"model" cities

Brasilia

Milton Keynes

Carcassonne

street grids

Design

Learn more online:
en.wikipedia.org/wiki/Architecture
www.architecture.com/Explore/Home.aspx

Real Places to Visit:
Arkitektur- och designcentrum, Stockholm, Sweden
Deutsches Architekturmuseum, Frankfurt, Germany
The Lighthouse, Glasgow, UK
Chicago Architecture Foundation, Chicago, USA
Netherlands Architecture Institute, Rotterdam, Netherlands

Coincidental Connections - Round 8

And here is the last round of Coincidental Connections!

If you have missed the background information for Coincidental Connections, please go back to page 75.

The 8th Round

Horizontal: .... - .... - ....

Left-hand side: ....

Right-hand side: ....

Roll the dice once more for the Round 8 Block theme:

1. Use only curved lines.
2. Do not use curved lines.
3. Use only straight lines.
4. Do not use straight lines.
5. Use curved and straight lines.
6. Joker - Choose from 1, 2, 3, 4, or 5.

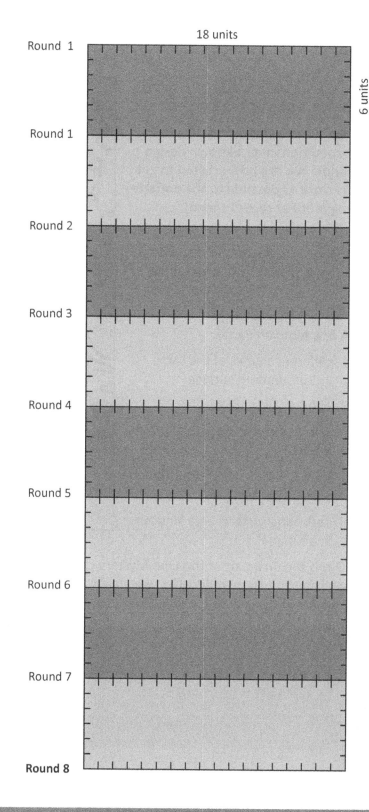

18 units

6 units

Round 1
Round 1
Round 2
Round 3
Round 4
Round 5
Round 6
Round 7
Round 8

Coincidence is the only legitimate sovereign in the universe.

Napoleon Bonaparte

Line Drawing Mystery - Part 6

The Line Drawing Mystery is just that - a line drawing of a mysterious motif chopped into 6 pieces with only a minimum of information on colour values and textures.

Please go back to Part 1 for details on this series of exercises.

Always remember that this is an expedition into unknown design lands. You are not required to get as close as possible to the underlying motif at record speed!

The orientation shown is not necessarily the orientation from the original picture. The parts of the Line Drawing Mystery will appear in a random order.

A few hints on Part 6:

1 different shades of the same colour, smooth surface

2 light and hazy colour

3 fairly dark, not smooth, natural surface

4 medium dark, fairly smooth and man-made surface

5 reflecting surface, very smooth, man-made

This is the final part of this Line Mystery Quilt Project. You now have all the components to make a small wall hanging. Remember: The objective is not to get as close as possible to the underlying picture, but to enjoy the voyage into the unknown!

> In nature, we never see anyhting isolated, but everything in connection with something else.
>
> Johann Wolfgang von Goethe

If you are wondering what could be behind this Line Mystery:

Go to page 133!

Bonus Exercise: Music

Inspired by the chapter on architecture which strictly speaking is not an era of art history either but an encompassing theme, there were so many ideas on music that we have included a previously unpublished bonus chapter.

Get in the Mood - Music x 3

Normally, quilters are inspired by what they see. But what about what we hear?

Choose three pieces of music which are as different as possible. You might even select a piece from a musical style which you don't usually like. Close your eyes and listen to the music. Focus on the rhythm of the individual pieces.

Now make a sketch for each musical piece which portray the rhythms - as you heard, sensed and understood them.

Put aside your sketches for a few days. Then take them up again and think about ways to create a design from them.

There is no noise.

Only sounds.

John Cage

If you like this exercise, you might also like the first My Year of Design book from where this exercise was taken and slightly adapted to our purposes here.

More information on the book can be found in the appendix on page 132 or on our website:

www.quilt-around-the-world.com

Dig Deeper - Music

Association

clef

scales

major

minor

cord

Musical pieces are ordered sound events which are created with the help of musical instruments, electrical sound generators and the human voice.

One, two, many

In music there are unison pieces and songs, duets and multi-voice works such as pieces for a chorus or a canon.

How could you portray a duet in a quilt? If you like, look for a duet which you like, listen to it in peace and quiet, perhaps with closed eyes. Which colours and shapes do you see before your inner eye?

What would a choral or a canon look like in fabric?

multi-voice - unisonous

Questions

octave

In what ways does music influence our daily life? How does it represent what humans think and believe?

harmony

rhythm

tonal system

Life is Rhythm

Look for any musical piece and focus on the rhythm. Listen to the piece several times and try to portray the rhythm with geometrical shapes (lines, rectangles, circles...).

Put aside the sketch for a few days. Then take it up again.

Can you create a design for a textile piece?

Research

Mozart

Vivaldi

John Cage

Beethoven

Haydn

Bernstein

Débussy

Chopin

Verdi

Dvorak

Who is your favourite composer? Has your research influenced your preferences?

Selection

Acoustic Colour

Put very simply, one could say that every instrument has a very characteristic acoustic colour which is why different instruments sound different even when playing the same note.

Choose three different instruments (ideally from different families of instruments, e. g. one wind instrument, one keyboard instrument and one string instrument) and imagine their sounds. If you have the possibility, listen to corresponding music.

Try to describe the acoustic colours with a few adjectivs. Then think about which actual colour you would assign the instruments.

opera

rondo

Lied

party hit

Design

More information online:
en.wikipedia.org/wiki/Music

Real places to visit:

Cité de la musique, Paris, France

Museo nazionale degli strumenti musicali, Rome, Italy

Haus der Musik, Vienna, Austria

Musikinstrumentenmuseum Basel, Switzerland

Country Music Hall of Fame, Nashville, USA

Appendix

All Worksheets

Sources

Research:

Use the internet. Especially Wikipedia is a valuable source as well as websites of (art) museums.

Consider visiting museums and also libraries if it fits into your schedule.

If you are generally interested in art and history of art, you might want to purchase a book which gives you an overview.

Selection:

Let the results of the previous stages simmer for a few days.

Then take out your Dig Deeper Worksheet again.

Highlight the aspects which you find most interesting/intriguing/inspiring.

Have a look at your "Where am I today" mind map from time to time.

Finally, decide on one aspect to translate into a design.

Design:

Questions:

Ask yourself as many questions as possible and write them down.

Consult your collection of free associations and focus on areas which seem unclear.

You might want to focus on art and craft and contemplate why certain objects were made and for whom.

Title:

Associaton:

Note down whatever comes to mind first!

Whatever you write down need not be "correct" or historically accurate! The more spontaneous, far-flung, even erratic your first associations are, the more interesting your journey will be.

Use mind maps and sketches - whatever is best for you to allow ideas and images to flow.

Get in the Mood - Colour Play

1 | a | | | b | c | d | | e | | f | g |

Colour fields b, d and g with your least liked colour. Colour the other fields with its two triadic partners on the colour wheel.

2 | a | | | b | c | d | | e | | f | g |

3 | a | | | b | c | d | | e | | f | g |

4 | a | | | b | c | d | | e | | f | g |

Get in the Mood - Complex Grids

Worksheet

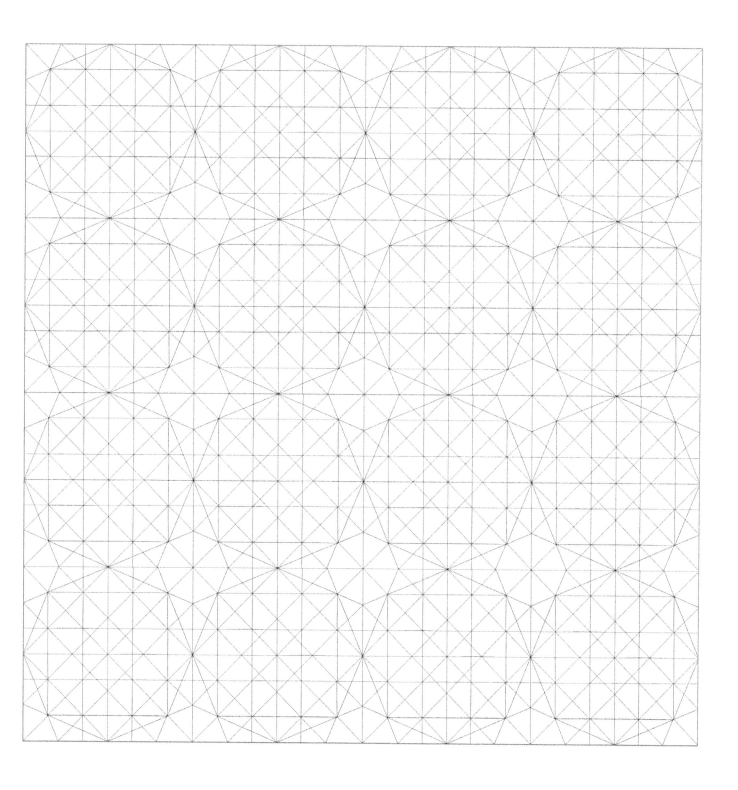

Get in the Mood - Complex Grids

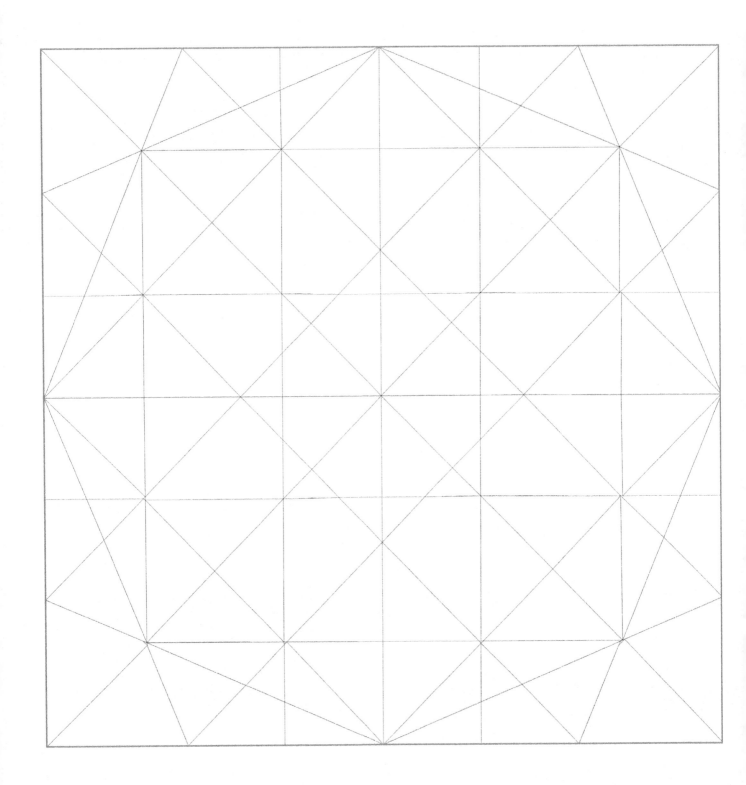

Coincidental Connections Worksheet

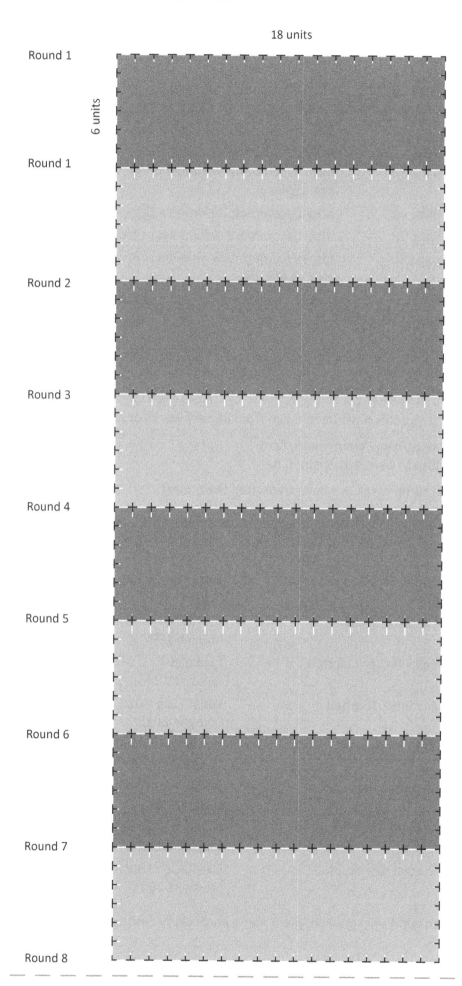

18 units

6 units

Round 1

Round 1

Round 2

Round 3

Round 4

Round 5

Round 6

Round 7

Round 8

Picture Credits

page 19	https://commons.wikimedia.org/wiki/File:Mona_Lisa,_by_Leonardo_da_Vinci,_from_C2RMF_retouched.jpg (picture in public domain)
page 20	https://commons.wikimedia.org/wiki/File:Durer_Young_Hare.jpg (picture in public domain)
	https://commons.wikimedia.org/wiki/File:Sandro_Botticelli_-_La_nascita_di_Venere_-_Google_Art_Project_-_edited.jpg (picture in public domain)
page 36	https://commons.wikimedia.org/wiki/File:Eye_of_Horus_bw.svg (GNU Free Documentation License)
page 43	https://commons.wikimedia.org/wiki/File:Bauhaus-Signet.svg (picture in public domain)
page 78	https://commons.wikimedia.org/wiki/File:07leucip.jpg (picture in public domain)
page 80	https://commons.wikimedia.org/wiki/File:Plan_de_Versailles_-_Gesamtplan_von_Delagrife_1746.jpg

Other Sources

The quotes have been taken from literary works or researched on the following internet pages:

http://www.brainyquote.com
https://www.aphorismen.de

In some cases, we have translated the quotes.

The weblinks listed in the individual chapters aside, the following books have been very helpful when working on My Year of Design content and exercises:

Barrucand/Bednorz	Maurische Architektur in Andalusien Cologne 1992
Caruana, Wally	Die Kunst der Aborigines Munich 1997
Fahr-Becker, Gabriele	Jugendstil Cologne 1996
Farthing, Stephen	Kunst - Die ganze Geschichte Cologne 2012
Rud, Morgens	Der Teppich von Bayeux Copenhagen 2004
Tavernier, Ludwig	Ausstellungsstraße Barock & Rokoko Mailand 1999
Vincent, Robert	Geometry of the Golden Section Marseille 2011
Wetzel, Christoph	Das Reclam-Buch der Kunst Stuttgart 2001

Iin addition, some chapters name particularly recommended books.

What Comes Next?

More My Year of Design

The My Year of Design series is growing! On these two pages you will find all the books and activities which would like to invite you to ever more new journeys of thinking and making.

Should you have questions on the publications and the activities, feel free to e-mail us at:

info@quilt-around-the-world.com

We would also welcome any feedback on this book.

If you are interested in other Quilt around the World activities, please go to page 136.

My Year of Design ZWEI - The exhibition CD

The exhibition CD for My Year of Design TWO contains all pieces on show which were made based on the online version of My Year of Design TWO. Moreover you will find the tutorials for all the Mystery blocks on this CD.

Requirements: PC with CD-ROM drive and software to display photos and PDF documents

8.00 €

Available in our online shop
www.quilt-around-the-world.com/Webshop

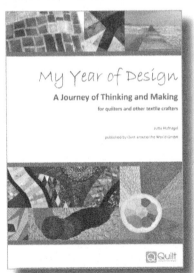

My Year of Design

The first My Year of Design book is a collection of design exercises inviting you on a journey of thinking and making. This journey will lead you off the beaten paths of quiltmaking and will help you see the world around you with different eyes.

My Year of Design started as a weekly online series in 2014. On more than 140 pages, you will find over 60 completely revised exercises, thereof 5 bonus exercises previously unpublished, inspirational quotes of famous writers, painters, sculptors and other clever people, interviews with participants from around the world giving you insight into their approaches to their own design adventure, and a gallery showing pieces resulting from the online version of My Year of Design.

For technical reasons, this book is not available in international bookshops. Please order from our online shop.

22.90 €
ISBN: 978-3-7392-0070-5
148 pages

My Year of Design 2GO

My Year of Design 2GO, the "little one" in the My Year of Design series, invites you every day to play with exciting and inspiring design exercises - only for in between chores or on the road when shopping, travelling, going to work. And this quite deliberately with this small workbook which fits into every handbag. You only need a pencil to be very much "offline", but using all your senses for taking in and being inspired by what surrounds us every day.

9,90 €
ISBN: 978-3-7431-1238-4

My Year of Design THREE

My Year of Design THREE (MYoD3) is our third journey of thinking and making and offers a comprehensive online course in design for quilters and other textile lovers. Design is a language - a visual language which can help convey messages and which can help to create work which is visually and sensually pleasing.

MYoD3 continues the tradition of the previous MYoD publications in challenging you with playful, amusing and sometimes unexpected exercises. These exercises are accompanied by inspirational pictures, background information (you could call this "design theory" if you were so inclined) and feedback on the pieces you produce based on MYoD3.

MYoD3 is divided into three modules of six chapters each. Each month, you will receive a detailed feedback on at least one piece you have made based on the respective exercises.

You will need a PC with Internet access and software to display PDF documents.

30,00 € (per module. Important: Limited number of participants!)
More information: www.quilt-around-the-world.com/en/MYoD3

49mysteries

Our popular Block Mysteries are back! 49mysteries will bring you a new exciting and fun block riddle each week and the respective detailed sewing tutorial a week later – for a whole year!

Moreover, you will have access to the new Quilt around the World Academy tutorials which will support you in translating your own designs into fabric!

You will need a PC with internet access and software to display PDF documents.

25,00 €

More information: www.quilt-around-the-world.com/en/49mysteries

25connections

And for all fans of Coincidental Connections we have a very special "web freebie" for you: Every other week, we will publish the instructions for designing one of 25 blocks which you can make into an extraordinary quilt sampler in the course of a year.

Free!

More information: www.quilt-around-the-world.com/en/25connections

Here is the solution to the Line Drawing Mystery:

It is the **"Walking Man" by Jonathan Borofsky** which you will find in Leopoldstrasse in Munich, Germany, in front of the main entrance of the reinsurance company Munich Re (close to the U-Bahn station Giselastrasse).

en.wikipedia.org/wiki/Walking_Man_(sculpture)

Other Activities in Print

Water for the World - IBS2 Quilts on Tour

"Water is the elixir of life" was the motto of the 2nd International Block Swap organized by Quilt around the World in 2013/14.

This catalogue accompanies the International IBS2 Travelling Exhibition and features selected water quilts designed and sewn by quilters from around the world, who participated in the block exchange and are now proud to present their finished works at various quilt shows in Germany, Europe and the USA.

15,90 €

Paperback
136 pages
Bilingual version - German/English
ISBN: 9-783734-790706

Making Waves - Water for the World Quilt

Besides a detailed report on the International IBS2 Travelling Exhibition, this book presents in 23 chapters all the wave panels of the large community quilt "Water for the World", which was crafted with the blocks donated by the IBS2 participants. In addition, all submitted motifs are shown, a total of 170 blocks of quilters from 20 nations.

Each chapter also features one exemplary block pattern for a certain water theme and/or sewing technique as a source of inspiration for own quilt projects.

22,90 €

Paperback
152 pages
Bilingual version - German/English
ISBN: 978-3-7431-6258-7

In the Sun 1 and 2 - IBS3 Quilts on Tour

"In the Sun" was the motto of the 3rd International Block Swap organized by Quilt around the World in 2015/2016.

The Travelling Exhibition which is shown at events in Europe and in the USA comprises over 80 textile works which were made from the 270 different sun blocks, designed and crafted by quilters from 22 nations.

17,90 € each

Paperbacks
144/132 pages
Bilingual versions - German/English

Please order via the webshop at www.quilt-around-the-world.com.

Books by Other Authors

Wort und Faden - Word and Thread

Heidemarie Mönkemeyer

With the help of fabrics, lace and edgings - old, stashed and left behind - the textile artist Heidemarie Mönkemeyer tells the forgotten stories of women who lived long ago and commemorates them in word and thread.

This personal artist portrait gives you a comprehensive insight into the works of Heidemarie Mönkemeyer. The 35 pieces show the development of her textile pictures and the accompanying texts and poems since 2008.

18,00 €
ISBN: 978-3-7412-2234-4

Water Variations
Inspiration for Textile Surfaces

Michaela Mosmüller

This book is dedicated to the textile translations of different aspects of the element water. Detailed step-by-step tutorials offer an exciting and entertaining approach to textile surface design for beginners. At the same time, advanced quilters find lots of inspiration for their own experiments in the unusual and unconventional techniques.

22,90 €
ISBN: 978-3-7431-2678-7

Most books are available through book shops, well stocked quilt shops or directly via our website:

www.quilt-around-the-world.com

When ordering from our webshop, please take into account that we are a very small company and cannot compete with the big players, neither regarding shipping costs nor delivery times.

By buying books from us, you are supporting future Quilt around the World activities.

Moreover, for each copy sold directly through our webshop or at quilt shows, we donate 1 € to the international humanitarian organisation Doctors without Borders.

About Quilt around the World

Quilt around the World is an innovative, independent and international online portal for patchwork and quilting. Besides online and book publications on patchwork and quilting themes, the focus of Quilt around the World is the organization of international quilt activities, such as block swaps, challenges and online classes on the design of quilts and related objects.

Should you be interested in our work, please visit our website at:

www.quilt-around-the-world.com

or e-mail us at:

info@quilt-around-the-world.com

Snailmail Address

Quilt around the World GmbH
Groß-Nabas-Straße 3
81827 München
Deutschland

Please note that this is merely an office and not a shop with regular opening hours. Should you like to meet us in person, you could do this either at a quilt show or by arranging an individual appointment with us. In both cases we recommend you to send an e-mail well in advance.

4th International Block Swap

Start date: 1 May 2017

Motto: Back to Nature

Deadline: 28 February 2018

All information:
www.quilt-around-the-world.com

Friends and Supporters

9 783743 126763